LUNCH IS IN THE BAG!

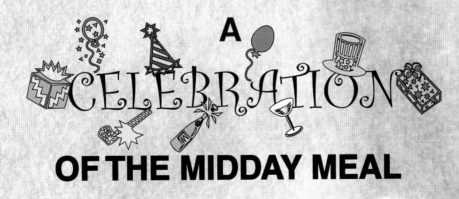

A

CELEBRATION

OF THE MIDDAY MEAL

By Marion O. Celenza

To Cathy and Chip, Paula and Fred, Linda and Alan....
and to all future chefs who grasp the baton. Feed the world!

Cover Design by Irene Lang
Interior Design by Chip Celenza, Irene Lang
Sketches and Photos by Marion O. Celenza
Editorial Assistant: Annemarie Mascolo
Editor: Chip Celenza
Printed by Cherry Lane Litho

CATALOGING IN PUBLICATION DATA
Celenza, Marion O.
   LUNCH IS IN THE BAG!
   1. Cooking

ISBN: 978-0-9791953-1-0

LCCN: 2008903871

TABLE OF CONTENTS

A Celebration of
The Midday Meal

INTRODUCTION

LUNCH IS IN THE BAG! is a midday celebration. Its innovative format continues my spectacular MENU LOG: A Collection of Recipes as Coordinated Menus which was published in 2004.

LUNCH IS IN THE BAG! creates 52 luncheon menus, which are special, different and exciting to the taste. Each menu is coordinated to marry Soup or Salad to Entrée to Dessert, in a seasonal ambiance.

Designating your lunch to a certain time-slot requires flexibility and imagination, not to mention a certain degree of self-determination. We've become completely unstructured: lunch in the left side top drawer of the work desk (bologna on rye if you're lucky!); a hot dog dressed in peppered soot from a city vendor; a mushy peanut butter and jelly sandwich AND an apple (from Mom), or "I just don't know what this mess is platter" on the school menu; yogurt and crunchies (where's that spoon?); a loaf of crusty bread, a hunk of Jarlsberg Swiss AND a bottle of California red — on a blanket at the beach or at the park (you should be so fortunate!).

Or, if you're as most of today's society — a soda from a vending machine and a bag of chips will suffice.

LUNCH IS IN THE BAG! sets the table for a special lunch. Say, on a weekend, a "free day", a special get-together at home with friends. You'll find sections on Brunches and Sandwiches, Lunches for Two, Dressings, Sauces and Gravies — as well as suggestions for a picnic in the park.

So! Relax — smell the succulent aromas from your kitchen or grill — and enjoy
    LUNCH IS IN THE BAG! A CELEBRATION OF THE MIDDAY MEAL.

MARION O. CELENZA

FALL–WINTER

Mixed Greens Salad
Chicken Piccata
Rustic Pasta
Citrus in Marsala

❄❄❄❄❄❄❄❄❄

MIXED GREENS SALAD

2 cups escarole
2 cups romaine lettuce
1 cup chicory or frisée

Rinse greens in cold water; drain in colander (prep early and cover bowl with plastic; refrigerate). Tear greens into bite-size pieces. Place in large salad bowl. Add Italian Dressing (see page 173) and toss to mix. Serve immediately. Servings: 4-5.

…………………………..

CHICKEN PICCATA
(May be prepared in advance; cover and refrigerate. Warm covered with foil
    at 250° F, 20-25 minutes.)

4 thin boneless chicken breasts (one for each serving) – wash in cold water, pat dry with
    paper towel
1 large white onion, thinly sliced
3 garlic cloves, chopped
canola oil for sautéing (a thin film on bottom of skillet)
juice of 2 lemons
$\frac{1}{4}$ cup dry vermouth
1 cup hot water into which 2 chicken bouillon cubes have been mashed
$\frac{1}{4}$ cup flour (enough flour and a taste of black pepper to dredge chicken)

On a sheet of waxed paper, add enough flour, seasoned with black pepper to coat chicken breasts. Heat oil in skillet to 320° F; dredge chicken in flour mix; sauté chicken 2-3 minutes on each side. Remove chicken to platter. Use an oven-proof deep dish. Brown sliced onion and garlic in same skillet; add chicken stock to skillet; gradually add flour, stirring constantly to thicken the gravy; scrape bottom of skillet; stir in vermouth and lemon juice. Pour gravy over chicken in platter. Cover dish loosely with foil and warm in low oven (250° F) for 10 minutes. If prepping in advance, decant gravy into a small container. Pour over chicken before warming in slow oven 250° F for 20 minutes (lay a loose foil cover over dish). Serves 4.

…………………………..

RUSTIC PASTA
(Assemble just before serving.)

1 carrot, pared and chopped
$\frac{1}{2}$ red bell pepper, remove seeds, thinly slice
$\frac{1}{2}$ green bell pepper, remove seeds, thinly slice
2-4 mushrooms, scrub, thinly slice
4 slender stalks asparagus, rinse, cut into one-inch pieces
1 small onion, chopped
2 garlic cloves, chopped
1 heaping tbsp. fresh parsley, chopped
1 tsp. salt
$\frac{1}{4}$ tsp. black pepper
2 tbsp. flour
2 tbsp. olive oil
1 cup fat-free evaporated milk
1 cup grated Parmesan cheese (divide into 2 parts)
8 – 10 oz. pasta (rotini or bowties)

In a small saucepan, simmer onion and garlic in olive oil until light brown. Stir in flour to form a smooth paste. Continue to simmer. Add milk, stirring constantly. When slightly thickened, stir in salt, pepper, parsley and $\frac{1}{2}$ cup grated cheese. Cover; keep warm, stirring occasionally. Meanwhile, prepare pasta. In large pot, bring 3 quarts water to a full boil (add salt to water, if desired). Cook pasta al dente, according to directions on package. Drain pasta in colander and turn into large (at least 2 $\frac{1}{2}$ qts.) oven-proof serving bowl. Add all vegetables; pour cheese sauce over pasta and vegetables and mix thoroughly. Sprinkle rest of cheese over top. Serve immediately. (4-6 portions)

....

CITRUS IN MARSALA
(May be prepared early on the day. Refrigerate.)

2 large grapefruit (remove sections to mixing bowl)
2 seedless oranges (remove sections to mixing bowl)
juice of 1 lemon
1 Kiwi for garnish (peeled, sliced into 4 rounds; add to mix)
$\frac{1}{2}$ cup Marsala wine (or Madeira or Sherry)

Gently separate fruit segments; try to keep slices whole. Divide grapefruit and oranges among 4 (8-oz.) glass dessert bowls. Stir strained juice of lemon into Marsala. Pour equally over 4 bowls of fruit. Garnish with slice of Kiwi. Chill until serving. Serves 4.

❀❀❀❀❀❀❀❀❀

Parmesan Chicken
Cassoulet
Vineyard in the Snow

❄❄❄❄❄❄❄❄❄

PARMESAN CHICKEN
(May be prepared early on the day or day before; refrigerate and warm thoroughly.)

4 – 6 chicken cutlets, thick, skin removed
1 cup grated Asiago cheese
1 cup grated Parmesan cheese
2 eggs (or $\frac{1}{2}$ cup egg substitute)
1 $\frac{1}{2}$ cups milk (or fat-free evaporated milk)
2 cups plain bread crumbs
$\frac{1}{2}$ cup chopped parsley
2 garlic cloves, minced
1 tsp. salt
$\frac{1}{4}$ tsp. black pepper
1 can (about 1 lb.) unseasoned artichoke hearts
2 tbsp. olive oil to coat 9x12 non-stick pan
extra oil for sprinkling

Preheat oven to 400° F. Grease bottom of 9x12x3 baking pan with olive oil. Beat eggs and milk together. In a separate bowl combine crumbs, cheeses, parsley, garlic, salt and pepper. Dip chicken breasts in egg-milk mix; coat in bread-crumb mix. Arrange chicken in prepared pan. Add artichoke hearts on top of chicken. Sprinkle with olive oil. Bake in preheated oven 400° F for 45 minutes or until chicken is tender and thermometer registers 170° F. Serves 4-5.

....

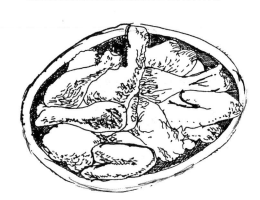

CASSOULET

2-lb. can cannellini beans, rinsed in cold water, drained (or you may use 1 lb. dried beans, presoaked and cooked as directed on package)
1 large onion, thinly sliced
$\frac{1}{2}$ cup canned whole tomatoes, mashed
4 garlic cloves, chopped
4 slices lean bacon
$\frac{1}{4}$ cup plain bread crumbs
2 links fennel sausage
1 pt. stock, prepared by adding 1 pint water to cooking pan and scraping bottom of pan
1 tsp. salt
$\frac{1}{4}$ tsp. black pepper
$\frac{1}{2}$ tsp each: oregano, basil, crushed bay leaves
3 cups baby spinach, washed, drained – uncooked

In a large skillet, sauté bacon until crisp. Remove and drain on paper towels; set aside. In same skillet, brown sausages. Remove sausages to cutting board and slice into one-half inch chunks. Set aside with bacon. Add one pint hot water to pan; scrape bottom of pan as you simmer. Add onion, tomatoes, garlic, herbs and seasonings. Simmer for 10 minutes. In a 2-quart casserole dish (preferably Pyrex or oven-proof) pour cooked beans and sausage. Pour tomato mix over the beans. Stir to mix. Crumble bacon and spread bacon and crumbs over bean mix. Bake in slow oven 250° F for 25 minutes. Serve warm over platter of uncooked baby spinach. Serves 4 – 5.

………………………………..

VINEYARD IN THE SNOW

2 tbsp. sherry
2 cups seedless red grapes, rinsed and drained
1 cup seedless green grapes, rinsed and drained
1 cup chopped walnuts
2 cups whipped heavy cream (add 1 tsp. vanilla extract when whipping into stiff peaks)
chocolate curls to decorate

Have ready: grapes and nuts in large serving bowl. Sprinkle sherry over grapes and nuts. In a mixing bowl, beat cream and vanilla at high speed until stiff peaks form. Fold whipped cream into nuts and grapes. Decorate with chocolate curls. Refrigerate until serving. Serves 4-5.

❄❄❄❄❄❄❄❄❄

Salad of Greens and Carrots
Pork and Apricots
Portobello Arraganate
Almond Slices

❋❋❋❋❋❋❋❋❋

SALAD OF GREENS AND CARROTS

1 cup each: red leaf lettuce, green leaf lettuce, arugula, baby spinach (rinsed and drained)
1 cup carrot curls
2-3 small mushrooms, chopped
½ cup blueberries
Honey Mustard Dressing (see page 173)

In a large salad bowl, toss greens, carrots and blueberries to mix. Refrigerate until
serving. Then, add Honey Mustard Dressing; toss and serve. Serves 4-5.

……………………………..

PORK AND APRICOTS
(May be prepared and baked in advance. Warm in slow oven until well heated.)

4 boneless loin pork chops, 1-inch thick, trimmed
½ cup apricot jam with fruit, 4-6 fresh apricots, halved OR 1 sm. jar apricot halves
1 cup corn flake crumbs
4 tbsp. honey mustard spread
olive oil to coat pan

Preheat oven to 350° F. Lay sheet of waxed paper on cutting board. Spread half of the
crumbs on sheet. Lay the chops on the crumbs. Stir mustard into the jam; spread
one tbsp. jam mix on top side of each chop. Use your hands to pack the remainder of
crumbs on top of the fruit-coated chops. Oil-coat a 7x9 non-stick pan. Place the
prepared chops in the pan. Add apricot halves around chops in pan. Place a sheet of foil
loosely over the pan like a tent. Bake in preheated oven 350° F for 25- 30 minutes.
Do not overcook. Crust will be light golden brown. Serves 4.

……………………………..

PORTOBELLO ARRAGANATE
(May be prepared in advance and warmed just before serving.)

12 oz. Portobello mushrooms, sliced
   $\frac{1}{2}$-inch thick (about 15-18 slices)
$\frac{1}{8}$ cup balsamic vinegar
$\frac{1}{4}$ cup olive oil
$\frac{1}{2}$ cup unseasoned bread crumbs
2-3 garlic cloves, minced
$\frac{1}{4}$ tsp. black pepper

dash of salt
2 tbsp. oregano
3-4 whole bay leaves
$\frac{1}{4}$ cup grated sharp provolone cheese
1 red Bell pepper, seeded, vertically
   sliced (about 1 dozen slices)
more olive oil for sprinkling

Preheat broiler to 500° F. Rinse and drain mushrooms. Pat dry with paper towels. Pour olive oil and balsamic vinegar over bottom of 10-inch round metal pie pan. Coat each slice of Portobello in this mix as you lay them side-by-side, in a circle in the pan. Garnish the mushrooms with strips of red pepper. In a small bowl, make a mix with crumbs, pepper, salt, garlic and oregano. Sprinkle this mix over the mushrooms and peppers. Scatter grated provolone over this mix. Lastly, lay the bay leaves, here and there and sprinkle 1-2 tablespoons of olive oil. Broil at 500° F, 5 inches below burner for 2-3 minutes or until cheese is lightly browned. Serves 4-5.

……………………………..

ALMOND SLICES
(May be prepared a week in advance.)

$\frac{3}{4}$ cup canola oil (or 1 cup Smart Balance spread; or 1 cup butter)
1 $\frac{1}{2}$ cups granulated sugar
4 eggs, beaten (or 1 cup egg substitute)
4 cups flour
2 cups chopped almonds
1 tsp. baking powder
1 tsp. vanilla extract
1 tsp. almond extract

Preheat oven to 375° F. In a large bowl, cream oil (or butter), sugar and eggs. Add rest of ingredients and knead until smooth. Add more flour if necessary. Form 2 long logs, 3x12 inches, on a floured board. Grease a large cookie sheet. With 2 spatulas, carefully transfer the logs to the cookie sheet. Bake in preheated oven 375° F for 10 – 12 minutes until golden brown. (Do not turn off oven.) Remove cookie sheet from oven to cool. Transfer logs to cutting board; cut slices $\frac{3}{4}$-inch thick. Place cookies, flat side down, onto greased cookie sheet. Re-bake at 375° F for 3 more minutes. Remove from oven. Cool thoroughly and store in airtight tin. Makes about 4 dozen. Serve with fresh strawberries and a cup of espresso.

❁❁❁❁❁❁❁❁❁

Salad with Nuts and Fruits
Veal with Pineapple
Sweet and Sour Rice
Vanilla Ice Cream Almandine

❁❁❁❁❁❁❁❁❁

SALAD WITH NUTS AND FRUITS

4 cups escarole, trimmed, rinsed, drained, cut into bite-size
1 cup dried cranberries
1 cup chopped red delicious apples with skin
1 cup slivered almonds
Balsamic/Olive Oil Dressing (see page 173)

In a large salad bowl mix escarole, cranberries, apples, almonds. Refrigerate until serving. Add dressing, toss and serve. Serves 4.

……………………………..

VEAL WITH PINEAPPLE
(If preparing ahead of time, use oven-proof platter.)

6 – 8 veal cutlets, pounded
4 – 6 mushrooms, washed, sliced
2 tbsp. olive oil
$\frac{1}{4}$ tsp. black pepper
dash of salt
4 slices canned pineapple, halved (save juice)
$\frac{1}{2}$ cup sweet wine (marsala, sherry, vermouth)

Sprinkle salt and pepper on veal. Heat oil in large skillet (about 320° F) and sauté cutlets, one or two at a time, for 2 minutes on each side. Remove them to a large serving platter. Repeat this process until all of the cutlets are cooked. Add mushrooms to skillet and sauté for 2 minutes. Remove to platter with cutlets. Add pineapple to skillet and heat on each side. Arrange pineapple and mushrooms on top of veal. Turn up heat under skillet. Add wine to skillet as you quickly scrape bottom of pan with spoon, forming a light sauce (about 30 seconds). Pour hot sauce over the platter and serve immediately. Or, cover with foil. Heat thoroughly in low oven just before serving. Serves 4-5.

……………………………..

SWEET AND SOUR RICE

1 cup brown rice
1 cup pineapple juice, 2 tbsp. brown sugar
$\frac{1}{2}$ cup water
$\frac{1}{2}$ cup cider vinegar
2 chicken bouillon cubes, 1 tsp. salt
1 carrot, pared, chopped
1 tbsp. chopped ginger root
1 large celery stalk, peeled, chopped
2 tbsp. white raisins, chopped

Pour liquids into 2-quart saucepan; bring to a boil. Add and mash bouillon, stirring to
mix. Add rice. Stir and simmer, covered, for 20-25 minutes, or until some of liquid is
absorbed. Add celery, carrots, ginger root and salt during last 5 minutes of cooking.
Simmer until most of liquid has been absorbed. Stir in raisins. Serves 4-6.

…………………………..

VANILLA ICE CREAM ALMANDINE

4-5 servings vanilla bean ice cream
4-6 crumbled almond cookies
4-6 tbsp. amaretto liqueur
1 cup chopped almonds with skins
(whipped cream, optional)

Scoop one portion of ice cream per serving into each dessert bowl. To each portion, add
cookies and liqueur, and top with chopped almonds. Add a dollop of whipped cream.
Serves 4-5.

❄❄❄❄❄❄❄❄

Beef Barley Soup
Stuffed Fish Fillets with Vegetables
Date-Nut Bread
Spicy Apple Slices

❄❄❄❄❄❄❄❄❄❄

BEEF BARLEY SOUP

2 qts. beef stock (Beef stock may be prepared by adding a beef shin bone to 2 quarts
 boiling water, and simmering for $\frac{1}{2}$ hour; or, by mashing 8 beef bouillon cubes into
 2 qts. of boiling water; or, by using 1 qt. canned beef consommé plus 1 qt. water.)
1 cup barley
2 carrots, pared, chopped
1 large onion, chopped
2-3 small tomatoes, skinned and mashed (It will be easier to skin a tomato, if you let it
 rest in boiling water for 2 minutes; then, drain and peel with fingers.)
$\frac{1}{2}$ cup celery, chopped
3-4 mushrooms, washed, chopped
1 large all-purpose potato, pared, cubed
$\frac{1}{2}$ tsp. black pepper
1 bay leaf
1 tsp. oregano
salt to taste (If using canned consommé or bouillon, additional salt may be unnecessary.)

Add barley to simmering stock. Cook, covered for 30 minutes. Add all vegetables, herbs
and spices and simmer for 1 hour. Serves at least six.

…………………………………..

STUFFED FISH FILLETS WITH VEGETABLES

4-5 large fish fillets (flounder or sole)
2 cups cleaned medium shrimp and bay scallops, mixed
2 links sweet Italian sausage (remove casing; chop the meat; sauté in small pan brushed
    with olive oil)
1 tbsp. chopped parsley
1 tbsp. chopped onion
½ cup unseasoned bread crumbs
salt, black pepper, to taste
½ cup egg substitute; or 2 eggs beaten with 1 tbsp. water
4-6 baby bella mushrooms, scrubbed, sliced
1 small red Bell pepper, thinly sliced
1 ½ doz. thin asparagus stalks, trimmed, washed
½ cup water
olive oil to coat non-stick pan, 9x13x1 ½
4-5 small metal skewers

Preheat oven to 400° F. Wash fillets; pat dry with paper towels. Lay fish on glass cutting
board. In a small bowl, mix shrimps, scallops, cooked sausage meat, parsley, onion,
crumbs and seasonings. Sprinkle egg mix over filling and mix thoroughly. Divide filling
into 4-5 parts (for each fish portion), and pack the mix into the center of each fillet. Roll
the fillets (probably 3 turns) and fasten with a skewer. Coat a 9x13 pan with olive oil.
Pour ¼ cup water into pan. Place pan on large stove burner and turn up to high heat.
When water boils, add mushrooms, peppers and asparagus. Lower to a simmer for
2 minutes. Remove pan from burner. Stir vegetables and spoon aside to one end of pan.
With spatula, carefully lay fish fillets onto baking pan. Spoon vegetables over the rolled
fish. Bake in preheated oven at 400° F for about 20 minutes, occasionally spooning
vegetable sauce over fish. Serves 4-5.

....

DATE NUT BREAD

2 cups boiling water	2 tsp. vanilla extract
2 ½ cups pitted dates, chopped	3 cups flour
2 tsp. baking soda	dash of salt
½ cup granulated sugar	2 tbsp. canola oil
2 beaten eggs or ½ cup egg substitute	1 cup chopped pecans

Preheat oven to 350° F. Grease and flour 2 loaf pans, 5x7x3. Pour boiling water over dates in a small bowl. Mix and set aside. Combine baking soda, sugar, eggs, oil, vanilla and salt. Add flour, dates, water and nuts. Pour batter into prepared pans. Bake at 350° F for 1 hour or until a toothpick comes out clean. Serve with cream cheese and sliced spicy apples (see recipe below). Serves 6-8.

……………………………..

SPICY APPLE SLICES

2-3 Granny Smith apples, washed, cored
½ cup brown sugar
1 tsp. cinnamon
¼ cup lemon juice

Pour lemon juice into a small wide dish with sides. On a sheet of waxed paper, spread brown sugar mixed with cinnamon. Thinly slice off both ends of apples. Slice each apple into 4-5 circles, dependent on size of apple. Dip both sides of apple slices into lemon juice; coat with sugar mix. Arrange apple slices on a platter, cream cheese in center, and serve with slices of Date-Nut Bread. A cup of Earl Grey tea will "hit the spot".

❋❋❋❋❋❋❋❋❋

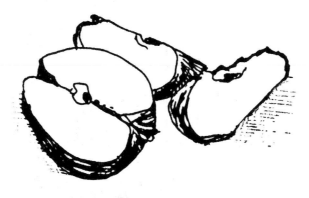

Fennel Salad
Pasta a la Sicilia
Veal Piccata
Stewed Fruit

❊❊❊❊❊❊❊❊❊❊

FENNEL SALAD

2 large fennel bulbs, trimmed, quartered, cut off center rind
1 cup mixed olives, pitted: Sicilian, Calamata, Greek
2 large red peppers, roasted with cloves of garlic (see note on how to roast peppers *)
Balsamic Dressing (see page 173)

On a large flat serving dish, attractively arrange fennel, peppers and olives. Sprinkle with Balsamic Dressing just before serving. Serves 4-5.

*"How to Roast Peppers"
(1) If you are roasting more than 2 peppers, preheat oven to 450° F. Lay 4-6 peppers on a cookie sheet lined with a sheet of foil. Remove the seeds and ribs before roasting by coring the peppers. Insert a clove of peeled garlic into the cavity of each pepper. Roast peppers 15 – 20 minutes on each side (turn twice). The skin will char. Remove the tray from the oven, wrap the peppers in the foil, and allow them to steam, covered, until they are cool enough to handle. Then peel off the skin (starting from blossom end).
You may serve them (with the garlic) as a whole pepper or sliced into 2-inch strips.
(2) Or: If you're roasting 1 or 2 peppers, use a long-handled fork and char the peppers over an open flame, turning them every 2-3 minutes, until skins are blackened. Then, proceed to remove skin as in "method (1)". Also, cut off ends and discard seeds and ribs.
(3) Or: Broil peppers by laying them on a cookie sheet lined with foil as in "Method 1". (You may remove seeds before broiling.) Broil about 3 inches from heat, turning peppers every 5 minutes for 20 minutes or so, until skins are charred. Proceed as directed in "Method (1)". (If preparing chiles, use protective gloves.)
Whichever method you choose, when broiling or charring do not leave procedure unattended.

………………………………..

8 – 10 oz. linguini pasta (whole wheat pasta suggested)
1 can (1 lb.) artichoke hearts, unseasoned (in water), quarter each artichoke heart
1 cup assorted pitted olives (in oil)
1 red pepper, roasted, cleaned, sliced in slivers
1 small can anchovies , chopped
1 small onion, chopped
2 garlic cloves, minced
$\frac{1}{4}$ tsp. black pepper
1 tsp. salt
pinch of hot pepper flakes (to taste)
$\frac{1}{4}$ cup vodka
2 tbsp. olive oil
$\frac{1}{2}$ cup grated Asiago cheese
2-3 leaves fresh basil, torn into pieces (for garnish)

Brown garlic, onion, and artichoke hearts in olive oil in a small skillet. Remove from heat; stir in olives, red pepper slivers, and anchovies. Set aside. Cook pasta, al dente, as directed on package. Drain the pasta immediately and pour into a large serving bowl. Add vodka, black pepper, salt, hot pepper flakes to artichoke mix. Pour sauce mix over pasta in bowl; sprinkle cheese over pasta mix and toss with 2 large spoons. Garnish with basil leaves. Serve immediately. Serves 4 as a side dish.

………………………………..

VEAL PICCATA

2 tbsp. flour
$\frac{1}{2}$ tsp. salt
$\frac{1}{4}$ tsp. black pepper
6-8 veal cutlets, pounded thin
$\frac{1}{4}$ cup olive oil
$\frac{1}{4}$ cup dry white wine
1 lemon, thinly sliced
$\frac{1}{4}$ cup fresh parsley, chopped

SAUCE:
1 tbsp. olive oil
1 egg yolk or $\frac{1}{4}$ cup egg substitute
$\frac{1}{4}$ cup dry white wine
juice of 1 lemon

Preheat skillet to 340° F degrees. Combine flour, salt and pepper on a sheet of waxed paper to coat veal. Sauté veal in $\frac{1}{4}$ cup olive oil until brown: about 2-3 minutes on each side. Add wine, lemon slices and parsley and simmer, covered, for 10 minutes. Remove veal to serving platter and keep warm. Discard the slices of lemon.
Prepare sauce: Heat 1 tablespoon olive oil in same skillet. Beat egg yolk with wine and lemon juice; slowly stir wine mix into skillet. Stir constantly. Cook over low heat, stirring, until sauce is thickened and hot. Pour over veal. Serves 4.

....

STEWED FRUIT

1 $\frac{1}{2}$ cups fresh cranberries, rinsed, drained (usually sold in 12 oz. package)
1 cup granulated sugar
1 cup orange juice
1 cup seedless green grapes, washed and drained
1 large navel orange; cut out fruit from rind with serrated knife, and chop orange sections
     into small pieces
1 tbsp. candied ginger, chopped
1 tbsp. candied ginger, chopped (for garnish)

In a 2-qt. saucepot, mix cranberries, orange juice and sugar. Cover, bring to a boil over high heat. Lower heat and simmer, covered, for 10 minutes. Remove from heat and transfer to a large, decorative serving bowl. Add and stir in grapes, orange chunks and 1 tablespoon of candied ginger. Cover with plastic and chill for several hours or overnight. Garnish with candied ginger just before serving. Serves 6.

❄❄❄❄❄❄❄❄❄

Pear and Gorgonzola Salad
London Broil Teriyaki
Asian Rice
Ginger Muffins

❄❄❄❄❄❄❄❄❄

PEAR AND GORGONZOLA SALAD

4 cups mixed: red leaf and green leaf lettuces, wash, drain, tear or cut into bite-size
¼ lb. Gorgonzola cheese, crumbled
2 large Bartlett pears
Honey Mustard Dressing (see page 173)

Combine lettuces and crumbled cheese into a large salad bowl. Set aside in refrigerator. In a small jar, prepare Honey Mustard Dressing. Halve and core pears and cut each half into 4 slices. Divide the slices among 4 salad plates; arrange 4 pear slices around the rim of each plate. Shake the jar of dressing thoroughly and pour one-quarter cup on the bowl of lettuce. Add the crumbled cheese and toss to mix. Spoon the greens mix in the center of each salad plate. Sprinkle additional dressing over the plates. Serve promptly. Serves 4.

....

LONDON BROIL TERIYAKI
(Sauce may be prepared ahead of time and refrigerated.)

1 cup soy sauce (use reduced salt variety)
¼ cup olive oil (or peanut oil)
¼ cup apricot jam
4 tsp. cornstarch
¼ tsp. black pepper
1 tsp. minced garlic

2 lbs. top round (for London broil, 1 ½-inches thick)
1 dozen mushrooms, no stems, washed and drained
2 dozen cherry or grape tomatoes, washed and drained
4 long metal skewers

Preheat grill or broiler to 500° F. Prepare teriyaki sauce: in a small saucepan, combine soy sauce, oil, jam, cornstarch, pepper and garlic. Stir to blend and bring to a boil over medium heat, stirring continuously. Remove from heat. Brush the meat with the sauce. Grill steak 4 inches from heat; turn once and brush other side with sauce.
Broil 5-7 minutes per side for rare; 8-10 minutes for medium-rare; 11-13 minutes for well-done. Meanwhile, divide mushrooms and tomatoes evenly (3 mushrooms, 6 tomatoes) and thread them onto 4 skewers. About 4 minutes before steak is done, brush skewered vegetables with sauce, and broil or grill them for 2 minutes longer. Transfer the meat to a large platter and slice the steak thinly, diagonally across the grain. Serve with skewered vegetables. Serves 4 generous portions.

....

ASIAN RICE

1 cup white rice
1 onion, chopped
½ green pepper, diced
1 tbsp. soy sauce
1 tbsp. canola oil
2 cups chicken consommé

Cook rice in consommé for 15 minutes. In a small pan, sauté onion and pepper with canola oil until tender (do not brown). Mix with rice in rice pot. Add soy sauce and simmer a few minutes longer until most of liquid is absorbed. Serves 4-6.

…………………………..

GINGER MUFFINS

1 ½ cups flour
¼ tsp. salt
¼ tsp. cinnamon
¼ tsp. nutmeg
¼ tsp. cardamom
½ cup molasses

¼ cup canola oil
1 egg or ¼ cup egg substitute
1 tsp. baking soda
1 tsp. powdered ginger
¼ cup brown sugar
½ cup boiling water

Preheat oven 400° F. Grease medium-size muffin tin (12 muffins). Sift together into a large bowl: flour, baking soda, salt and spices. In another bowl, combine molasses, brown sugar, oil and boiling water. Add liquid mix to dry mix a little at a time. Beat in the egg; do not over beat. Batter may be lumpy (that's okay). Spoon batter into greased muffin cups. Bake in center of preheated oven at 400° F for 20-25 minutes. Serve warm. Makes 10-12 muffins.

❀❀❀❀❀❀❀❀❀

Spinach and Endive Salad with Mandarin Oranges
Beef and Pork Stew
Cherry Noodle Pudding

❋❋❋❋❋❋❋❋❋

SPINACH AND ENDIVE SALAD WITH MANDARIN ORANGES

4 cups baby spinach, rinsed, spun dry
2 Belgian endives sliced thin crossways
1 small can Mandarin oranges, drained
Bleu Cheese Dressing (see page 175)

In a large salad bowl, combine spinach, endive and oranges. Prepare Bleu Cheese Dressing in a small jar. Add to salad just before serving and toss. Serves 4.

……………………………..

BEEF AND PORK STEW
(May be prepared in advance and reheated.)

1 lb. beef cubes
1 lb. lean pork cubed
2 carrots , pared, cut into 1-inch chunks
1 onion sliced
1 large stalk celery, peeled, cut into chunks
2 tbsp. olive oil

$\frac{1}{2}$ cup red table wine (Burgundy is suitable)
$\frac{1}{4}$ cup tomato purée, dissolved in 1 cup water
6 small mushrooms, rinsed and quartered
1 tsp. salt
$\frac{1}{4}$ tsp. black pepper
1 tsp. each: dried basil, oregano, thyme

8 oz. wide egg noodles cooked separately as directed on package; after cooking toss with 2 tablespoons olive oil just before serving, as an accompaniment to the stew.

In a 4-quart stew pot, brown the meat and vegetables in 2 tablespoons olive oil. Add the tomato sauce/water, wine, seasonings and herbs. Blend the sauce into the stew; cover and gently simmer for 1 hour. Serves 4-6 with a side of wide noodles.

……………………………..

CHERRY NOODLE PUDDING

$\frac{1}{2}$ lb. medium noodles
$\frac{1}{4}$ lb. cream cheese
$\frac{1}{2}$ cup sugar
$\frac{1}{3}$ cup milk
1 lb. cottage cheese
1 pt. sour cream
1 $\frac{1}{2}$ tsp. vanilla extract
$\frac{1}{2}$ tsp. cinnamon
3 eggs or $\frac{3}{4}$ cup egg substitute
1 can (about 20 oz.) cherries used for pie filling

Preheat oven to 350° F. Grease 9x13 pan. Prepare noodles as directed on package. Rinse in cold water and drain. Place noodles in a large mixing bowl. In a small bowl, mash cream cheese; add all other ingredients, except eggs and cherries. Mix into noodles. Beat eggs, one at a time, and stir into noodle mix. Pour this mix into prepared greased 9x13 baking pan. Bake at 350° F for 30 minutes. Remove from oven and spread cherries over the top; bake an additional one-half hour. Serves 8.
(You may not wish to serve noodles with the stew if you have added Cherry Noodle Pudding to this menu.)

❋❋❋❋❋❋❋❋❋

Romaine with Apples, Red Onion and Black Olives
Curry Veal
Rice and Beans
Candy-Cake

❄❄❄❄❄❄❄❄❄

ROMAINE WITH APPLES, RED ONION AND BLACK OLIVES

4 cups romaine lettuce, washed, drained
1 ½ doz. oil-cured olives, pitted
1 small red onion, sliced thin
1 crisp apple (Granny Smith, Fuji, Braeburn), cored, cubed (do not pare)
Apple Cider Dressing (see page 177)

In a large, decorative salad bowl, mix romaine, onion and pitted olives. Do not add cubed apple until ready to serve. (You may briefly store cut apples by sprinkling them with lemon juice; cover tightly with plastic wrap; otherwise, apple will brown.) Cover bowl with plastic wrap and refrigerate until ready to serve. At that time, mix in cubed apple and dressing. Serves 4-6.

……………………………..

CURRY VEAL

1 ½ lbs. veal cutlets
1 cup chopped onion
4 tbsp. olive oil (divided in half)
2 garlic cloves, minced
2 tbsp. curry powder
2 tbsp. cornstarch

1 tsp. salt
¼ tsp. black pepper
¼ tsp. cumin
¼ cup dry white wine
1 cup chicken stock (prepared by
      mashing 1 chicken bouillon cube in
      1 cup boiling water)

Preheat oven to 325° F. Slice cutlets into bite-size; set aside. In a large skillet, heat 2 tablespoons olive oil and sauté onions and garlic. Combine curry powder and cornstarch and stir into 1 cup stock. Stir this mix into skillet with onions. Blend and cook slowly until onions become transparent and sauce is slightly thickened. Season with salt, pepper and cumin. Stir in wine. Transfer sauce to a baking dish with a cover. Sauté veal in the remaining 2 tbsp. oil until golden. Add veal to curry sauce. Cover dish and bake in oven 325° F for 25-30 minutes. Baste occasionally with sauce; you may have to add more wine to have sufficient sauce. Keep warm, covered, until ready to serve. Serves 4-5. Accompaniments: small dishes of shredded coconut, chopped peanuts, raisins, chutney.

…………………………..

RICE AND BEANS

1 cup brown rice
2 cups water
1 can (1 lb.) dark red kidney beans, rinsed, drained
1 small can (8 oz.) pineapple in chunks with juice
1 cup Curry Sauce (see page 180)

In covered pot, cook rice in 2 cups water for 25 minutes, or until most of liquid is absorbed. Stir in red beans and pineapple chunks with juice. Set aside. Prepare Curry Sauce. Pour 1 cup Curry Sauce into rice and beans mix, stirring to blend. Transfer to serving bowl; keep warm. Serves 4-6.

…………………………..

CANDY-CAKE
(Prepare day before. Sprinkle with confectioners' sugar just before serving.)

½ cup canola oil or 8 tbsp. butter
½ cup granulated sugar
3 eggs or ¾ cup egg substitute
2 cups sifted flour
2 tsp. baking powder
½ tsp. cinnamon
¼ tsp. salt

¼ cup chopped candied fruit mix
1 tbsp. orange rind. grated
½ tsp. orange extract or
    Grand Marnier liqueur
3 tbsp. water
confectioners' sugar for dusting

Preheat oven to 300º F. Grease 8-inch heart-shaped baking tin (or an 8-inch layer cake pan). In a large bowl, cream oil (or butter) with sugar. Beat in eggs, one portion at a time. Sift flour with baking powder, cinnamon and salt into the butter mixture. Stir in chopped candied fruits, orange rind, extract and water. Mix thoroughly. Pour the batter into the prepared pan and bake 20 minutes at 300º F. Raise the oven temperature to 425º F and bake for another 15-20 minutes, or until a toothpick comes out clean. Remove cake from pan when cooled. Store wrapped in foil until ready to serve. Dust with confectioners' sugar just before serving. Serves 6-8.
(This menu is suitable for a Valentine's Day luncheon.)

❀❀❀❀❀❀❀❀❀

Cabbage Slaw with Oranges
Paella
Banana Bread

❄❄❄❄❄❄❄❄❄

CABBAGE SLAW WITH ORANGES

3 cups finely shredded green cabbage (center of cabbage) or ready-prepared cabbage slaw
½ cup dried cranberries
1 large navel orange, peeled, divided into segments, chopped ½-inch pieces
1 carrot, shredded
Cole Slaw Dressing (see page 177)

In a large salad bowl, toss to mix: shredded cabbage, dried cranberries, orange chunks and shredded carrot. Prepare Cole Slaw Dressing and add to salad bowl. Toss well to mix. Serves 4-5.

…………………………..

PAELLA

2 boned, skinned chicken breasts, sliced in one-inch strips
4 links sweet Italian sausage, cut into one-inch chunks
1 lb. raw, large shrimp, shelled, cleaned
½ dozen cherrystone clams in shell, scrubbed
½ dozen large mussels in shell, scrubbed
1 large onion chopped
2 garlic cloves, minced
1 green pepper, chopped
(1 small chile, seeds removed, chopped – wear plastic gloves) – optional
2 large tomatoes, peeled, chopped (drop tomatoes into boiling water for 2-3 minutes; skin will peel off easily)

1 sm. can (16 oz.) black beans, rinsed, drained
1 sm. can (16 oz.) peas, rinsed, drained
1 pt. chicken broth, canned; or, mash 2 chicken bouillon cubes into 1 pt. hot water
1 tsp. saffron threads
1 tsp. black peppercorns
½ tsp. salt
1 tsp. oregano
1 tsp. Hungarian paprika
¼ cup olive oil
1 cup long grain rice
2 cups chicken broth

Ingredients can be prepared the day before. Assemble all ingredients in groups; prep shellfish, wrap in plastic and refrigerate; package meats in plastic, refrigerate; when using, wash chicken strips and pat dry with paper towel; remove beans and peas from cans and rinse – store in bowl; chop vegetables and store in bowl; refrigerate; store herbs and spices in plastic baggie.

In a very large paella pan or extra-large skillet brown chicken and sausages in one-quarter cup olive oil; add onion and garlic and brown. Add peppers and tomatoes; stir in broth, all herbs and spices, and the shrimp, mussels and clams. Cover and cook at medium heat for 10 minutes; turn off heat and set aside. Shellfish should open; discard clams and mussels that do not open.

Meanwhile, prepare rice: simmer rice in 2 cups chicken broth for 20 minutes. Now, return to the paella pan. Turn on heat to low; stir in beans and peas. With a large spoon and a spatula, gather the paella in the pan towards center. Spoon the rice in a ring around the paella. Return lid to paella pan and keep pan warmly heated. Serves 5-6, directly from the paella pan (or skillet).

………………………………..

BANANA BREAD (Prepare a day or two in advance.)

3 cups flour
1 tsp. baking soda
1 tsp. cinnamon
¾ tsp. salt
2 cups sugar
3 beaten eggs, or ¾ cup egg substitute

1 cup canola oil
2 cups mashed ripe bananas
2 tsp. vanilla
1 can (8 oz.) crushed pineapple, drained
½ cup chopped walnuts

Preheat oven to 350° F. Grease and flour 2 loaf pans, 5x7. In a medium bowl, combine flour, baking soda, cinnamon and salt. In a large bowl, blend thoroughly: sugar, eggs, oil, bananas and pineapple. Combine dry ingredients with sugar and egg mix in large bowl. Mix thoroughly; stir in nuts. Spoon batter into prepared pans and bake at 350° F for 50-60 minutes. Toothpick will come out clean. Remove bread when cooled. Wrap in foil; warm in foil before serving.

❀❀❀❀❀❀❀❀❀

Broccoli and Chick Pea Salad
Creole Lamb Chops
Cherry Coffee Cake

❄❄❄❄❄❄❄❄

BROCCOLI AND CHICK PEA SALAD

2 cups broccoli florets, rinsed, drained
1 25 oz. can ceci (chick peas), rinsed, drained
¼ tsp. dried hot red pepper flakes
2 garlic cloves, minced
1 sm. red onion, thinly sliced
2 tbsp. lemon juice
¼ cup fresh parsley, chopped
bed of Boston lettuce, washed, drained
Italian Dressing (see page 173)

In a large salad bowl, combine chick peas, onion, broccoli; sprinkle over bowl: minced garlic, hot pepper flakes, parsley and lemon juice. Cover bowl with plastic and refrigerate until serving. Prepare Italian Dressing in a small jar. Pour some dressing over salad just before serving and toss to coat vegetables. Prepare individual salad dishes with beds of Boston lettuce; spoon ceci salad onto the lettuce. Sprinkle more dressing over each salad. Serve immediately. Serves 4-6.

....

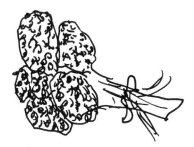

CREOLE LAMB CHOPS

4 – 8 loin lamb chops (depends on size), trimmed

4 tbsp. flour to coat chops

1 tsp. chili powder

$\frac{1}{2}$ cup red table wine

1 cup tomato purée

1 tbsp. oregano

1 tbsp. granulated sugar

2 Italian fryer peppers, seeded, sliced in strips

4 – 8 slices (1-inch thick) Portobello mushrooms, rinsed, drained

1 onion, thinly sliced

4 tbsp. olive oil

salt, black pepper to taste

Pour oil into a large skillet with a lid and oven-proof handle. Preheat oven 275° F. Spread flour, salt and pepper on a sheet of waxed paper. Coat the chops in this mix. In a small bowl, blend tomato purée, chili powder, oregano, sugar and red wine. Preheat skillet to moderate-high 340° F. Brown the coated chops in oil for a few minutes on each side. Transfer to plate. Brown peppers, onions and mushrooms for a couple of minutes; return the chops to skillet with vegetables. Pour the wine mix over the chops and vegetables in skillet. Cover skillet with lid and bake in a slow oven, 275° F for 20-25 minutes, depending on size of chops. Use meat thermometer: center of chops should be slightly pink. Serves 4-6.

…………………………..

CHERRY COFFEE CAKE
(Prepare a day or two in advance.)

$\frac{1}{4}$ lb. butter or Smart Balance spread

1 cup granulated sugar

2 eggs or $\frac{1}{2}$ cup egg substitute

$\frac{1}{2}$ cup low-fat milk

1 tsp. vanilla

2 cups flour

2 tsp. baking powder

TOPPING:

$\frac{1}{3}$ cup flour

$\frac{1}{4}$ cup granulated sugar

1 tsp. cinnamon

3 tbsp. butter or Smart Balance

1 can (1 $\frac{1}{2}$ lbs.) cherry pie filling

Preheat oven to 350° F. Grease and flour 8x11 pan. In a large bowl, blend butter, sugar, eggs and vanilla. Add flour mixed with baking powder alternately with the milk. Blend thoroughly. Pour half of the batter into the prepared pan. Spread cherry pie filling over batter; add remaining batter on top of pie filling.

TOPPING: In a small bowl, mix together with a fork: flour, sugar, cinnamon and butter until crumbly. Sprinkle this mix on top of batter and bake in preheated oven, 350° F for 1 hour. Serve warm from the pan.

❄❄❄❄❄❄❄❄❄

Red Cabbage, Cucumber, Radish and Tomato Salad
Beef Stroganoff
Crumbled Potato
Tipsy Apple

❋❋❋❋❋❋❋❋❋

RED CABBAGE, CUCUMBER, RADISH AND TOMATO SALAD

2-3 cups red cabbage, shredded
2 cucumbers, pared, sliced fine
1 dozen radishes, trimmed, sliced into rounds
2 tomatoes, yellow and red, sliced into rounds
4 scallions with greens, chopped
Lemon and Oil Dressing (see page 174)

In a small bowl, combine sliced cucumbers and radishes. Set aside. Line 4-5 small salad bowls with shredded red cabbage. Lay 2 slices tomatoes (yellow and red) on top of cabbage. Sprinkle each salad with some of the Lemon and Oil Dressing. Divide the cucumber mix into each salad bowl, over the tomatoes. Sprinkle chopped scallions on top. Drizzle more dressing over entire salad in bowls. Serve immediately. Serves 4-5.

…………………………..

BEEF STROGANOFF

2 lbs. boneless sirloin steak, sliced
  in thin strips
$\frac{1}{4}$ cup flour
dash of salt, $\frac{1}{4}$ tsp. black pepper
4 tbsp. canola oil
1 lb. mushrooms, rinsed, sliced
1 lg. onion, sliced

2 tbsp. Worcestershire sauce
1 tbsp. tomato paste
1 cup boiling water
1 tbsp. dry mustard
1 tsp. nutmeg
1 pt. sour cream

Spread flour mix on sheet of waxed paper. Have heat-resistant platter available. Preheat oil in large skillet to 320° F. Coat steak strips in flour mix; sauté in skillet for 1 minute on each side. Transfer steak to platter, arranging strips in an orderly fashion. Sauté mushrooms and onions; transfer them over the steak on the platter. Add tomato paste to boiling water in small pot; stir at low heat until smooth. Stir in Worcestershire sauce, mustard, nutmeg, sour cream. Pour over steak mix on platter. Serve warm. Serves 4-5.

…………………………..

CRUMBLED POTATO
(Prepare in advance. Heat in oven before serving.)

6 all-purpose potatoes, scrubbed, cut into chunks, do not pare
1 small onion, chopped
1 cup plain crumbs for stuffing (small cubes)
1 tbsp. chopped parsley
$\frac{1}{4}$ tsp. black pepper
1 tsp. salt
Hungarian paprika, to taste
2 tbsp. olive oil

In small bowl, mix parsley, salt, pepper into bread cubes. In large bowl, mix chunky potatoes, chopped onion. Add bread mix to potato mix. Sprinkle olive oil over potato-bread mix and with 2 large spoons, toss to coat with oil. Grease a non-stick pan, 9x13; preheat oven to 400° F. Pour bowl of potato mix into pan, and spread to fit entire pan. Sprinkle Hungarian paprika over pan (to taste). Bake in hot oven for 30 minutes; lay a sheet of foil over pan and continue to roast for another 15 minutes or until potatoes are tender when pierced with a thin skewer. You may store potatoes covered, in refrigerator. Heat thoroughly at 350° F, covered. Serves 4-5.

....

TIPSY APPLE
(May be prepared several days in advance.)

4-6 Rome Beauty apples, cored
2 cups either: pitted cherries, seedless grapes
$\frac{1}{4}$ cup brandy
4-6 tsp. butter or Smart Balance spread
6 oz. apple cider or apple juice
1 tbsp. cinnamon powder mixed into $\frac{1}{4}$ cup brown sugar

Preheat oven to 375° F. Soak cherries or grapes in brandy in a small bowl; refrigerate for 1 hour stirring a couple of times. Butter a round, deep casserole dish (no lid needed). Trim the skin off the top of each apple; arrange the apples to fit in a circle. Stuff apples with brandied fruit. Spoon 1 teaspoon butter on top of each apple; sprinkle generously with brown sugar-cinnamon mix. Dribble apple juice into centers of apples and onto bottom of casserole dish. You should have quarter-inch liquid at bottom of dish. If not, add a small amount of apple cider or juice. Bake in preheated oven, 375° F for 45-50 minutes, until you see cracks forming on skins. Insert a toothpick into an apple. If it slips in and out with ease, the apples are baked. Half-way through the timing, you may wish to lay a very loose foil tent over the apples. Do not over cook.
Serve warm or at room temperature. Serves 4-6.

✳✳✳✳✳✳✳✳✳

Three-Bean Salad and Pasta
Chicken Oregano
Almond Tart

❄❄❄❄❄❄❄❄❄❄

THREE-BEAN SALAD AND PASTA
(Prepare beforehand.)

1 can (1 lb.) red kidney beans, rinsed, drained
1 can (1 lb.) cannellini beans, rinsed, drained
$\frac{3}{4}$ lb. fresh green beans, trimmed, cut into pieces
8 oz. cut ziti (for salads), cooked al dente
2 garlic cloves, minced
$\frac{1}{4}$ red pepper, chopped fine
$\frac{1}{4}$ green pepper, chopped fine
$\frac{1}{4}$ cup chopped, pitted calamata olives
salt, black pepper to taste
olive oil to coat pan
$\frac{1}{4}$ cup grated Parmesan cheese
Parmesan Dressing (see page 176) (about 1 cup)

Pour Parmesan Dressing in a jar. Set aside.
Steam green beans for 3-4 minutes; set aside. Rub olive oil on bottom of 9x15x1 $\frac{1}{2}$-inch heat-resistant platter or pan. (This will be the serving platter.) Prepare pasta as directed on package. Rinse in cool water; drain. Place pasta into mixing bowl. Pour $\frac{1}{4}$ cup Parmesan Dressing over pasta; toss and mix thoroughly. Transfer to one-third area of serving platter (proceed in a horizontal pattern). Rinse and drain contents of each of the cans of beans. Arrange red kidney beans next to pasta, using 3 inches of space; place rinsed and drained cannellini beans next to them, using 3 inches of space; then, arrange green beans as the last horizontal column.

Over the pasta, sprinkle chopped, pitted olives; over red beans, sprinkle garlic; over cannellini, sprinkle chopped green pepper; over green beans, sprinkle chopped red pepper. Sprinkle black pepper and salt over the platter. Sprinkle remainder of the dressing over the beans, saving additional dressing over the pasta. Sprinkle grated Parmesan cheese over the entire platter. Warm in low oven, 200° F for 12-15 minutes. Serves 4-6.

....

CHICKEN OREGANO

4-5 chicken breasts, boned, skinned, washed and patted dry with paper towels
2 onions, sliced thin
2 red bell peppers, sliced thin
2 garlic cloves, minced
1 tbsp. oregano
1 tbsp. fresh, torn basil
1 tsp. salt
¼ tsp. black pepper
¼ cup olive oil
½ cup dry white wine

Have ready: large oven-proof serving dish. Pour oil in a large skillet. Brown onions and garlic on low heat for a few minutes. Add chicken, spooning onions over the chicken breasts as they cook. Turn up heat and brown chicken on each side (about 4-5 minutes each side). Reduce heat; remove chicken to serving platter; keep warm. Add red peppers to skillet and cook for a few minutes (you may have to add more olive oil). Add wine to skillet with onions and peppers. Cook and scrape bottom of skillet with spoon. Add oregano and basil; continue to scrape and stir as you bring wine mix to boil for 1 minute. Pour this sauce over the chicken in serving platter. Serve very warm, with a fresh, crunchy loaf of Italian artisan bread and a dry, white wine. Serves 4-5.

………………………………..

ALMOND TART
(Prepare a day or two in advance.)

4 eggs, or 1 cup egg substitute
1 cup granulated sugar
1 ¼ cups flour
½ cup softened butter or Smart Balance
   spread

½ cup water
2 ½ cups ground almonds
1 tsp. grated lemon rind
confectioners' sugar

Preheat oven to 350° F. Grease a 10-inch round cake pan. In a large bowl, beat eggs with sugar until light and fluffy. Add butter and mix until creamy. Add flour and water. With electric mixer at medium speed, beat for 15 minutes (do not under beat). Stir in almonds and rind. Pour batter into the prepared 10-inch pan, patting down the dough to fill the cake pan. Bake in preheated oven 350° F for 30-40 minutes until done. Test with toothpick to come out clean. Sift confectioners' sugar over tart when completely cooled. Cut into wedges. Serving suggestion: a fruity raspberry or apricot jam makes a tasty accompaniment. Serves 6.

❉❉❉❉❉❉❉❉❉

Artichoke Hearts, Fennel and Arugula Salad
Lasagna
Trifle

❊❊❊❊❊❊❊❊❊

ARTICHOKE HEARTS, FENNEL AND ARUGULA SALAD

1 can (1 lb.) artichoke hearts, unseasoned, cut in half
2 medium-size fennel bulbs, trimmed, sliced into $\frac{1}{2}$-inch rounds
4 cups arugula, trimmed, rinsed, drained
1 small red onion, sliced in thin rounds
1 dozen or more (to taste) assorted olives, pitted
1 tbsp. oregano
bunch of fresh basil, washed, drained
Balsamic Dressing (see page 173)

Prepare Balsamic Dressing; set aside. Arrange a bed of arugula on bottom of 4-5 salad plates; add 2-3 torn basil leaves to each salad. Layer in the following order: red onion on top of greens; a layer of fennel rounds; a layer of 2-3 pieces of artichoke hearts. Sprinkle oregano over each salad; sprinkle a couple of tablespoonfuls of Balsamic Dressing over each dish. Garnish each salad with olives and a sprig of basil. Serves 4-5.

…………………………..

LASAGNA

(May be prepared a day or two in advance. Wrap in plastic plus foil; refrigerate. Heat thoroughly in hot oven, 400° F, for 50-60 minutes or until top is golden and lasagna is thoroughly heated.)

1 lb. lasagna noodles (curly-edge); add 1 tsp. salt to pasta water
1 lb. sweet Italian sausage meat with fennel (remove casing; chop meat)
2 tbsp. olive oil
1 small onion, chopped
2 garlic cloves, chopped
4-6 mushrooms, rinsed, thinly sliced
1 can (1 pt.) chicken broth
1 cup dry white wine
$\frac{1}{4}$ tsp. black pepper
salt to taste
$\frac{1}{2}$ cup grated Parmesan cheese

SAUCE:
3 tbsp. olive oil
3 tbsp. flour
1 $\frac{1}{2}$ cups low fat milk; or fat-free evaporated milk
1 tsp. salt
$\frac{1}{4}$ tsp. black pepper
grated nutmeg
Parmesan cheese for sprinkling

Preheat oven to 400° F. Cook noodles al dente, as directed on package. Rinse noodles in cool water. Set aside in cool water; heat 2 tablespoons of olive oil in skillet. Sauté and stir chopped sausages for 2 minutes. Add onion, garlic and mushrooms to skillet and sauté for 2 minutes longer. Lower heat; add broth and wine; simmer for 10-15 minutes until sauce thickens. Set aside.

Oil a 9x12x3(4) casserole pan (used for lasagna).
Meanwhile, prepare the cream sauce by heating 3 tablespoons olive oil in saucepan; stir in flour; stir in milk, salt and black pepper. Cook on medium heat, stirring constantly to blend. Sauce will thicken. Set aside; keep warm and stir occasionally.

Line bottom of oiled casserole pan with noodles. Spoon into pan, one-half sausage-mushroom mix; add another layer of noodles; repeat with remainder of sausage mix. Top off with the final layer of noodles. Sprinkle one-quarter cup Parmesan cheese over each layer of sausages and mushrooms. Stir the warm cream sauce and pour over the casserole. Sprinkle with more cheese and some nutmeg. Bake in preheated oven at 400° F for 25-30 minutes or until top is golden and lasagna is thoroughly heated and bubbly. (If preparing beforehand, follow instructions as stated at beginning of recipe.) Serves 6.

…………………………………..

packaged small-size individual sponge cakes, 1 for each serving
4-6 macaroon cookies, crumbled
1 cup sherry
½ cup brandy
4-6 tbsp. slivered almonds
½ cup strawberry jam
2 cups fresh strawberries, sliced (save 4-6 large strawberries for garnish)
1 pt. heavy cream for whipping
1 pt. vanilla ice cream; or eggnog ice cream, if available

4-6 large (1 –pt.) dessert bowls

Place the sponge cakes, one to each dessert bowl. Add a layer of crumbled macaroons on top of each cake. Evenly distribute sherry over cakes and allow to rest for 10 minutes. Cover with a thick layer of strawberry jam. Add brandy to sliced strawberries. Refrigerate cakes and strawberries. Whip the cream to form stiff peaks. Refrigerate until ready to serve. At serving time, spoon one-half cup portion of ice cream over jam in each bowl. Divide sliced brandied strawberries over ice cream. Ladle generous dollops of whipped cream onto each portion, and garnish with almond slivers and 1 large strawberry. Serve immediately. Serves 4-6.

❆❆❆❆❆❆❆❆❆

Potage St. Jacques
Baked Fillet Sole
Stuffed Cookies

❄❄❄❄❄❄❄❄❄

POTAGE ST. JACQUES

½ lb. bay scallops, rinsed, drained
½ cup white wine
2 ½ cups water
1 bay leaf
1 tbsp. peppercorns
3 leeks, remove greens, trim bulbs
1 small onion, sliced thin
4 small potatoes, pared, sliced thin

4 tbsp. olive oil
2 ¼ cups evaporated milk
   (available fat free)
1 tsp. salt
¼ tsp. black pepper
⅛ tsp. cayenne pepper
1 pkg. (8 oz.) baked, seasoned croutons

Heat 4 tablespoons oil in a large soup pot. Lightly brown onions. Lower heat and add scallops, wine, water, bay leaf, peppercorns, leeks and potatoes. Simmer for 10-12 minutes. Stir in evaporated milk, cayenne, salt and pepper. Bring to a slow boil; then simmer for another 15-20 minutes. Mixture should thicken. Stir frequently as you cook. Serve hot with croutons. Serves 4-6.

....

BAKED FILLET SOLE

4-6 fillets of sole or flounder
   (not too large)
1 medium onion, sliced thin
¼ cup chopped fresh parsley
1 large carrot, pared, sliced very thin
10 oz. fresh baby spinach

4-6 small mushrooms, rinsed, sliced
½ lb. medium shrimp, cleaned
bread crumbs to coat fish
¼ lb. grated Swiss cheese
salt, pepper to taste
½ cup water, olive oil (about 3-4 tbsp.)

Preheat oven to 350° F. Line a large oil-coated casserole baking dish (this is the serving platter) with spinach, carrots, onions and mushrooms. Pour ½ cup water over this dish. Set aside. Spread crumbs on a sheet of wax paper. Coat fillets in crumbs. Lay coated fillet over spinach mix. Add shrimp over fillet. Sprinkle with salt and pepper. Mix parsley with grated cheese and spread over fish and shrimps. Drizzle a few tablespoons of olive oil over casserole. Bake in preheated oven 350° F for 25-30 minutes, until tops are lightly browned. Serves 4-6.

....

STUFFED COOKIES
(Prepare a day or two in advance; except for powdered sugar.)

DOUGH:
1 ½ cups sugar
5 cups flour
1 cup milk
2 tsp. baking powder
4 eggs or 1 cup egg substitute

FILLING:
½ cup bread crumbs
3 tbsp. grape jelly
¼ tsp. baking powder
2 tsp. cocoa
6 tbsp. light cream
½ cup chopped walnuts
1 tbsp. grated orange rind
confectioners' sugar for dusting

Preheat oven to 425° F. Grease 2 large cookie sheets. Prepare filling: combine all filling ingredients (from crumbs to orange rind) in a saucepan and cook over low heat for 10 minutes, stirring constantly. Set aside to cool. Prepare dough: combine all dough ingredients in a large bowl and work by hand to make a smooth dough. Knead on floured board. When dough is smooth, roll out one-quarter of dough on floured board, about ¼ -inch thick. (Keep unused portion covered.) Cut circles about 3 inches in diameter. Place a tablespoon of filling on each circle of dough, fold over, and pinch together the edges of the dough with the tines of a fork. Prick each crescent with a fork on top crust only. Repeat with rest of dough. Transfer cookies to prepared pans and bake in center of preheated oven 425° F for about 8 minutes, until cookies are pale brown. Remove from oven to thoroughly cool. Store cookies in a cool place, tightly wrapped. Dust with confectioners' sugar when ready to serve. Makes about 3 dozen cookies.

❀❀❀❀❀❀❀❀❀

Red Leaf Lettuce, Radish and Pine Nut Salad
Pork Chops with Figs in Madeira
Rice with Cashews
Apple Charlotte

❄❄❄❄❄❄❄❄❄

RED LEAF LETTUCE, RADISH AND PINE NUT SALAD

4 cups red leaf lettuce, rinsed, drained, torn in small pieces.
1 cup thinly sliced radishes, rinsed, and trimmed
$\frac{1}{4}$ cup pignola nuts, toasted lightly
Italian Dressing (see page 173)

In salad bowl combine lettuce and radishes. Sprinkle with pine nuts. Add dressing to salad just before serving. Toss well to mix. Serves 4.

………………………………..

PORK CHOPS WITH FIGS IN MADEIRA

4 thick boneless pork chops, trimmed
8 fresh figs or 1 jar (1 lb.) figs, drained
1 cup light red wine
1 tsp. sugar
1 tsp. ground cinnamon
1 tsp. whole cloves, 2 bay leaves
salt, pepper to taste
oil to coat pan

Preheat oven to 350° F. Use a shallow pan which is flame-proof (stove top) and oven proof. Coat pan with oil. On medium- high heat, sear chops on both sides (3 minutes on each side) in flame-proof pan. Remove from burner. In a small bowl, mix wine, sugar, cinnamon, salt, pepper and cloves. Leave figs whole and add them to pan with pork. Pour liquid over meat on dish. Lay bay leaves on top of chops. Cover with lid and bake in oven 350° F for 1 hour, adding a little more wine if necessary. Serve warm. Serves 4.

………………………………..

RICE WITH CASHEWS

1 slice bacon, cooked crisp, drained, crumbled
2 tbsp. olive oil
1 can (1 lb.) tomatoes, mashed with fork
1 cup long grain rice
1 small onion, chopped
1 garlic clove, minced
2 oz. cashew nuts
2 oz. raisins
1 small cayenne or chile pepper (to taste)
2 cups water
½ tsp. salt

Preheat over 350° F. In large skillet, cook bacon until crisp. Remove bacon; set aside. Add 2 tablespoons olive oil to the skillet. Heat oil mix and add rice, cooking on low heat, stirring occasionally, until rice is lightly browned. Add onion and garlic; stir and cook a few minutes longer. Add water, tomatoes, cayenne pepper (adjust the amount of pepper to satisfy how spicy hot you like it), nuts, raisins and salt. Mix well and turn into a covered 2-quart casserole. Cook in oven at 350° F for 15 minutes. Remove lid and continue to cook for an additional 10 minutes. Serves 6.

…………………………………..

APPLE CHARLOTTE

4-5 large Granny Smith apples, diced with skin
½ cup lt. brown sugar
1 tbsp. lemon juice
1 tsp. lemon rind, grated
2 oz. butter or Smart Balance spread
3 tbsp. apricot jam
¼ cup chopped dried apricots
2 tbsp. chopped almonds
4-5 small cookies, crushed (preferably almond or coconut)
½ pt. heavy whipping cream

Preheat oven to 375° F. In oven-proof bowl (you will serve from this bowl), combine diced apples, brown sugar, lemon juice and rind, jam, chopped apricots and chopped almonds. Dot with butter. Sprinkle crushed cookies over top. Bake in oven at 375° F for 35-45 minutes, until apples are soft. You may lay a piece of foil on top of bowl during the last 10 minutes of baking to prevent over-toasting the cookies. Serve warm. Just before serving, whip cream to stiff peaks; add a dollop of whipped cream to top each serving. Serves 4-5.

❄❄❄❄❄❄❄❄❄

Mixed Sausage Grill
Potato and Onion Pie
Cabbage Apple Slaw
Irish Soda Bread

❄❄❄❄❄❄❄❄❄

MIXED SAUSAGE GRILL

1 dozen links assorted sausages: veal, pork, spicy chicken, etc.

Preheat grill to 450° F. Lay sausages on metal pan. Grill on high heat, turning often to brown all sides. Transfer to serving platter lined with cabbage leaves. Serves 4-6.

………………………………..

POTATO AND ONION PIE
(Prepare a day in advance.)

1 9-10 inch ready-prepared pie crust, pricked with fork tines before filling
3-4 large all purpose potatoes, pared, sliced very thin
1 large onion, chopped
½ red pepper, chopped
½ green pepper, chopped
1 tsp. salt
¼ tsp. black pepper
2 tbsp. olive oil
1 tbsp. oregano
sprinkling of hot red pepper flakes
½ cup grated Irish brick cheese

Preheat oven to 450° F. In a large bowl, combine thinly sliced potatoes, onion, peppers, herbs, spices and cheese. Sprinkle oil over bowl and toss to coat. Have pie crust ready (prick with fork tines). Transfer contents of bowl to pie tin with crust. With your hands pack vegetables into crust. Bake in preheated oven 450° F for 10 minutes. Lower oven heat to 350° F and bake for 35-40 minutes longer, until potatoes are tender.
Serve in wedges. Serves 6.

………………………………..

CABBAGE APPLE SLAW

3 cups shredded cabbage
1 large carrot, pared, shredded
1 stalk celery, chopped fine
1 very small red onion, chopped fine
1 apple with red skin, chopped
1 tsp. salt

$\frac{1}{4}$ tsp. black pepper
2 tbsp. olive oil
$\frac{1}{4}$ cup cider vinegar
$\frac{1}{2}$ cup light Miracle Whip dressing
2-3 tbsp. lemon juice
1 tbsp. granulated sugar

In a large salad bowl combine cabbage, carrot, celery, onion and apple. In a small bowl, blend Miracle Whip, vinegar, lemon juice, oil, salt, pepper and sugar. Pour over vegetables in salad bowl. Toss with 2 large spoons to coat thoroughly. Serve on individual salad bowls, on cabbage leaves. Serves 4-6.

………………………………..

IRISH SODA BREAD

4 cups flour
$\frac{1}{4}$ cup sugar
1 tsp. salt
1 tsp. baking powder
1 tsp. baking soda
$\frac{1}{4}$ cup butter or Smart Balance spread

4 tbsp. caraway seeds
2 cups white raisins
1 $\frac{1}{3}$ cups low fat buttermilk
2 egg whites, beaten
milk

Preheat oven 375° F. Grease an 8-inch round loaf pan. Combine flour, sugar, salt, baking powder and baking soda. Cut in butter to make a coarse mealy dough. Stir in caraway and raisins. In a small bowl, beat egg whites and buttermilk together. Stir into flour mixture until moistened. Turn dough onto a floured board and knead lightly until smooth. Shape dough into a ball and place in a greased 8-inch round loaf pan. Cut a large cross about one-quarter inch deep on top of dough. Brush top with milk.
Bake at 375° F for 1 hour or until golden brown.
This menu is suitable for a St. Patrick's Day celebration.

❀❀❀❀❀❀❀❀❀

BEEF BARLEY SOUP, PAGE 10

Seafood Stew, page 110

8 Crostatas, page 145

THREE WRAPS, PAGE 163

CHERRY-RASPBERRY FRAPPE, PAGE 49

Salad Of Greens and Carrots, page 6

Frittatas (Omelets), page 168-9

BERRY FRUIT WALDORF, PAGE 129

ORANGE TAPIOCA, PAGE 103

VEGETABLE MEDLEY, PAGE 153

HEROES IN THE MAKING, PAGE 165

BUTTERNUT SQUASH SOUP WITH SAUSAGE, PAGE 128

PROSCIUTTO AND CHEESE QUICHE, PAGE 139

SPRING–SUMMER

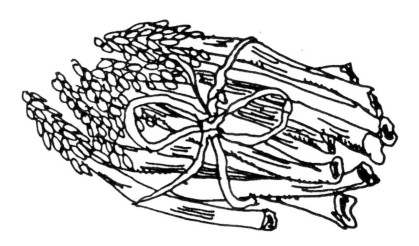

Spicy Vegetable Curry Soup
Wings and Ribs
Stir-Fry Vegetables
Allspice Pears

SPICY VEGETABLE CURRY SOUP

1 tbsp. olive oil
1 large onion, finely chopped
2-3 garlic cloves, minced
1 carrot, pared, finely sliced in rounds
2-3 all-purpose potatoes, skin removed, diced
1 can (1 lb.) chopped tomatoes in juice
4 cups water, 1 tsp. salt
1 can (1 lb.) ceci, rinsed, drained
1 tbsp. chopped cilantro
$\frac{1}{2}$ tsp. curry powder
$\frac{1}{2}$ tsp. or more (to taste) garam masala*

*GARAM MASALA is a blend of Indian spices. You may blend your own small jar of these spices for your spice rack.

4 oz. peeled cardamom seeds
2 tbsp. ground cinnamon
2 oz. ground cloves
4 tbsp. ground mace
4 tbsp. coriander seed
2 oz. whole peppercorns
3 tbsp. cumin seed
Grind these spices in a blender or spice grinder and save in a $\frac{1}{2}$-pint glass jar, tightly covered.

Heat olive oil in a large soup pot over medium heat. Add garlic and onion; stir, until onion starts to soften. Add carrots, potatoes, garam masala, curry powder and cook for 2 minutes. Add tomatoes, water and salt. Reduce heat, cover and simmer for 30 minutes, stirring occasionally. Add ceci and cilantro. Simmer for another 10 minutes. Serve hot. Serves 4-5.

…………………………..

WINGS AND RIBS
(Prepare in advance; wrap and freeze; defrost thoroughly; cover with foil; heat in moderate oven.)

1 dozen baby back spare ribs
1 dozen chicken wings, tips removed,
    washed and drained
4 tbsp. peanut oil
4 tbsp. soy sauce
4 tbsp. hoisin sauce
4 tbsp. honey
2 garlic cloves, minced
2 tsp. sesame seeds

MARINADE:
$\frac{1}{2}$ tsp. hot red pepper flakes
2 tsp. ground ginger
grated rind of 2 lemons
juice of 2 lemons

Wear protective gloves. In a small bowl, blend hot pepper flakes, ginger, lemon rind. Brush lemon juice on wings and ribs. Rub spice mix into wings and ribs. Set aside in refrigerator on waxed paper for 2-3 hours. Heat peanut oil in large shallow skillet or in a large wok. Add wings and ribs, a few at a time and sauté, turning them frequently for 5 minutes until golden (do not overcook). Drain on paper towels. Mix soy sauce, hoisin, honey, garlic and sesame seeds in a small bowl. Return wings and ribs to wok. Pour sauce over wings and ribs. Continue to cook for 5 minutes longer, turning wings and ribs often. Transfer them to a flat serving platter. Serve hot. Serves 4-5.

....

STIR-FRY VEGETABLES

1 small eggplant, remove skin, $\frac{1}{2}$-inch slices
6-8 broccoli florets, washed and drained
2 large Portobello mushrooms, rinsed, drained, sliced in $\frac{1}{2}$-inch pieces
$\frac{1}{4}$ cup olive oil
2 tbsp. balsamic vinegar
$\frac{1}{4}$ tsp. black pepper
1 tbsp. soy sauce

Prepare a marinade of oil, balsamic vinegar, soy sauce and pepper in a flat dish. Heat grill to high or set broiler to 500° F. Cook 4 inches from heat. Set out a large metal tray, 9x15; brush vegetable slices with marinade. Lay slices on metal tray and grill or broil at high temperature a few minutes on each side. Transfer to serving dish; pour remaining marinade over serving dish. Serve warm. Serves 4.

....

ALLSPICE PEARS

(Prepare a day in advance. Refrigerate.)

4 large ripe Bartlett pears, cored
1 cup orange juice
2 tsp. ground allspice
½ cup white raisins
2 tbsp. brown sugar
1 tbsp. grated orange rind

Preheat oven 375° F. Place the cored whole pears in a large oven-proof sauce pan or oven-proof casserole bowl. Stuff the pears with raisins. In a small bowl, blend juice, sugar and allspice. Pour over pears. Sprinkle each pear with orange rind. Set pan in preheated oven at 375° F. Bake for 45-50 minutes, until skin starts to crack or metal skewer easily slips out of pear. Pour syrup over pears when serving. Serves 4.

✿✿✿✿✿✿✿✿✿✿✿

Avocado Soup
Pork With Prunes or Cherries
Green Bean Salad
Oranges and Strawberries with Lime

❀ ❀ ❀ ❀ ❀ ❀ ❀ ❀ ❀ ❀

AVOCADO SOUP

3 cups water
1 onion, chopped
1 stalk celery, cleaned, chopped
1 carrot peeled, grated
4 garlic cloves, minced
1 bay leaf
1 tsp. salt
4 tbsp. lemon juice
$\frac{1}{4}$ tsp. black pepper
$\frac{1}{2}$ cup ground almonds
2 large ripe avocados
fresh cilantro, minced for garnish

Blend water, onion, garlic, carrot, celery and bay leaf in a 4-quart saucepot with lid. Add salt and pepper; cover, and simmer for 30 minutes. Cut avocados in half; discard stones and scoop out the flesh into a blender or food processor. Stir into soup base. Add ground nuts and lemon juice and blend thoroughly. This soup may be served chilled or warm. Sprinkle with chopped cilantro before serving. Add more salt and pepper to taste. Serves 4.

……………………………..

PORK WITH PRUNES (OR CHERRIES)
(Prepare marinade night before.)

4-5 thick loin pork chops, with bone, trimmed
juice of 3 limes
1 dozen garlic cloves, minced
4 tbsp. chili powder (mild to medium-hot)
2 tbsp. olive oil
1 large onion, chopped
2 $\frac{1}{2}$ cups chicken stock (canned consommé or mash 3 chicken bouillon cubes
    in 2 $\frac{1}{2}$ cups boiling water)
1 can (1 lb.) plum tomatoes, mashed with juice
2 dozen pitted dried prunes (2 dozen pitted cherries)
2 tsp. granulated sugar
$\frac{1}{4}$ tsp. ground cinnamon
$\frac{1}{4}$ tsp. ground allspice
$\frac{1}{4}$ tsp. ground cumin
$\frac{1}{2}$ - 1 tsp. salt (to taste)
warmed tortillas

On the day, preheat oven to 350° F. Prepare marinade night before: place the chops in a deep plate; combine lime juice, garlic, chili and salt. Pour over and under chops. Cover with plastic wrap and leave to marinate in refrigerator, over night. Next day, remove chops from marinade and wipe dry with paper towels. Reserve the marinade. Heat oil on medium heat in a flameproof casserole dish (with cover) and brown chops on both sides until golden. Add onions and reserved marinade, plus chicken stock. Cover and cook in preheated oven 350° F for 1-1 $\frac{1}{2}$ hours until tender. Spoon off any fat from surface of cooking liquid and add mashed tomatoes. Continue to cook in oven for 20 minutes. In a small bowl, combine prunes (or cherries), sugar and spices. Increase oven temperature to 400° F. Remove casserole from oven and pour prune-cherry mix over chops in sauce. Return covered casserole to oven for another 20 minutes, until juices have thickened. Remove from oven. Serve directly from casserole, spooning sauce over chops. Serve with warmed corn tortillas. Serves 4-5.

…………………………..

44

GREEN BEAN SALAD

1 lb. green beans, ends pinched, cut in half
1 small red onion, chopped
2 radishes, thinly sliced
4 tbsp. fresh cilantro, chopped
4 oz. feta cheese, crumbled
1 tsp. oregano (fresh or dried)
2 tbsp. red wine vinegar
4 tbsp. olive oil
2-3 ripe tomatoes cut into wedges or 6 quartered plum tomatoes
salt, pepper to taste

In a small vegetable steamer, steam beans in 1 inch of water for 4-5 minutes until just tender. Transfer drained beans to mixing bowl. Add onion, radishes, cilantro and feta. Toss to mix. Sprinkle oregano, pepper and salt over bowl. In a small bowl, mix vinegar and oil together and pour over salad. Toss gently to mix. Transfer to serving platter; surround with tomato wedges and serve at once or chill the dish until ready to serve. Serves 4-5.

....

ORANGES AND STRAWBERRIES WITH LIME

3 large navel oranges, slice off tops and bottoms, remove pith and peel, slicing from top to bottom in sections
1 dozen or more strawberries, hulled, washed and cut into slices, top to bottom.
grated rind and juice of 1 lime
1-2 tbsp. sugar
fresh mint to garnish

Place the prepared oranges and strawberries in a serving bowl. Sprinkle with lime juice mixed with sugar; sprinkle lime rind over bowl. Chill until serving time. Garnish with sprigs of mint before serving. Serves 4-5.

❁❁❁❁❁❁❁❁❁❁

Greens Salad with Pine Nuts and Olives
Turkey Tetrazzini
Fruit Compote

❀ ❀ ❀ ❀ ❀ ❀ ❀ ❀ ❀ ❀

GREENS SALAD WITH PINE NUTS AND OLIVES

2 cups greenleaf lettuce, rinsed and drained, torn into bite-size pieces
2 cups arugula, washed and drained
½ cup basil, washed and drained, torn into pieces
½ cup Sicilian olives, pitted
4 tbsp. pistachio nuts
2 garlic cloves, minced
1 tbsp. dried rosemary
Italian Dressing (see page 173)

In a large, decorative salad bowl, for serving, combine lettuce, arugula, basil, olives, nuts, garlic. Sprinkle rosemary on top. Refrigerate until serving. Mix Italian Dressing; pour on salad when serving; toss to mix. Serves 4-5.

…………………………..

TURKEY TETRAZZINI
(May be prepared in advance.)

4-6 turkey cutlets, skinned and boned
¼ cup slivered almonds
8 oz. wide noodles

SAUCE:
4 tbsp. olive oil
½ cup flour
1 tsp. salt
¼ tsp. black pepper
1 tbsp. Hungarian Paprika
1 tsp. curry powder
1 small onion, chopped
6 small mushrooms, washed, quartered
1 cup grated provolone cheese
1 cup turkey stock (or canned chicken consommé)
1 cup evaporated milk (available fat-free)

Preheat oven 350° F. Simmer turkey in 1 cup water until turkey is cooked. Remove meat to cutting board. Reserve stock for sauce. Slice cooked turkey into strips. Set aside on board. In a saucepan, heat oil and lightly brown onions. Lower heat; stir in flour, stock, milk, salt, pepper, paprika, curry and mushrooms. While stirring sauce over low heat, stir in cheese until melted. Sauce should be creamy and smooth. Divide sauce in half. In a bowl, coat turkey strips with half of the sauce. Set aside. Meanwhile prepare noodles as directed on package. Drain. In same noodle pot, add one half sauce to noodles and toss to coat. Pour coated noodles into oven-proof 3-quart casserole. Form a space in the middle of casserole, spreading noodles to form a ring. Pour turkey in sauce into center of this ring. Sprinkle slivered almonds over casserole. Bake in preheated oven 350° F for 20-25 minutes. Serves 4-5.

……………………………..

FRUIT COMPOTE

1 jar (1 lb.) fresh citrus fruit
1 package (1 lb.) dried pitted prunes
1 small can mandarin oranges
1 small can pineapple chunks
1 package (1 lb.) dried apricots

1 dozen strawberries, trimmed, washed
$\frac{1}{4}$ cup apricot brandy
$\frac{1}{2}$ cup walnut halves
fresh mint sprigs for garnish

Cook prunes and apricots in 2 inches water for 5 minutes. Remove from heat and drain. Set aside to cool. Discard water. In a large deep glass bowl, pour citrus fruits with juice, mandarin oranges in juice, pineapple juice, whole strawberries, prunes, apricots and walnuts. Add one-quarter cup brandy and stir to blend. Garnish with fresh sprigs of mint. Serves 8.

❀❀❀❀❀❀❀❀❀❀

Sweet-Sour Salad
Roast Salmon
Cherry-Raspberry Frappe

✿ ✿ ✿ ✿ ✿ ✿ ✿ ✿ ✿ ✿

SWEET-SOUR SALAD

2 cups shredded white cabbage
2 slender cucumbers, pared, thinly sliced in rounds
2 large tomatoes, sliced $\frac{1}{4}$-inch thick, in rounds
1 apple, cored, sliced into 8-10 narrow wedges, cut from top to bottom
2 navel oranges, slice off top and bottom, peel skin, slice into sections, top to bottom
4-5 cabbage leaves
juice of 1 lemon
juice of 1 lime

Insert cabbage leaves, one into each salad bowl (use as a cup to hold salad). Into each bowl arrange the vegetables in order: lay 1-2 slices of tomato on top of each leaf; arrange a layer of cucumber on each tomato; spoon $\frac{1}{2}$ cup shredded cabbage in center of bowl; squeeze juices into a cup and divide liquid over each mound of shredded cabbage. Garnish bowls with orange and apple sections.

....

ROAST SALMON

2 tbsp. olive oil
1 $\frac{1}{2}$-2 lbs. wild Alaskan salmon fillets, peel off skin (discard)
$\frac{1}{4}$ cup orange juice
finely grated rind of 1 orange
2 garlic cloves, minced
2 tsp. dried tarragon
salt to taste
$\frac{1}{4}$ - $\frac{1}{2}$ tsp. coarsely ground pepper
2 tsp. dill weed, chopped (or dried)

Preheat oven 475° F (or set grill to high). Grease non-stick pan with olive oil. In a small bowl mix marinade: oil, orange juice and rind, garlic, tarragon, salt and pepper and dill weed. Brush salmon on each side with marinade. Pour rest of marinade over salmon. Let salmon marinate for 1 hour at room temperature, turning it once or twice. Roast in preheated oven 475° F or transfer to a sheet of foil (with marinade) on grill, for 7-8 minutes. Turn salmon over and roast for another 7-8 minutes. (Fish is ready when it easily flakes when tested with a fork.) If grilling, carefully remove salmon to serving platter with 2 spatulas. Serves 4.

....

CHERRY-RASPBERRY FRAPPE

1 pt. raspberry sherbet
1 cup fresh Queen Anne or Bing cherries, washed, drained
$\frac{1}{2}$ pint fresh raspberries, rinsed gently, drained
$\frac{1}{4}$ cup brandy
$\frac{1}{2}$ pt. heavy whipping cream

Spoon a portion of sherbet into 4 individual glass, dessert bowls. Divide the raspberries over the sherbet bowls. Whip cream into peaks. Sprinkle 1 tablespoon brandy over each portion; spoon a dollop of whipped cream atop each and garnish with cherries. Serve immediately. This dessert must be prepared quickly. Serves 4.

❀❀❀❀❀❀❀❀❀❀

Hot and Sour Soup
Asian Salad
Teriyaki Chicken
Fresh Fruits in Ginger Sauce

❀ ❀ ❀ ❀ ❀ ❀ ❀ ❀ ❀

HOT AND SOUR SOUP

2 tbsp. cornstarch
4 tbsp. water
2 tbsp. soy sauce
3 tbsp. rice wine vinegar
$\frac{1}{2}$ tsp. black pepper
1 small fresh red chile, diced (wear protective gloves)
1 egg, beaten well or $\frac{1}{4}$ cup egg substitute

2 tbsp. peanut oil
1 onion, chopped
4 cups chicken consommé (canned, or mash 4 chicken bouillon into 4 cups boiling water)
$\frac{1}{2}$ cup shitake mushrooms, washed, drained

Stir cornstarch into water in a bowl to form a smooth paste. Add soy sauce, rice wine vinegar, pepper and chile to mix. Brown onions in oil in soup pot for 1-2 minutes. Stir in consommé, mushrooms, and bring to a boil. Cook for 15 minutes. Pour the cornstarch mix into the soup and cook, stirring, until soup thickens. As you are stirring, gradually drizzle beaten egg into the soup, to create threads of egg. Serve immediately. Serves 4.

……………………………..

ASIAN SALAD

12 spears slender asparagus, trimmed, rinsed
2 endives, washed, trimmed, sliced into $\frac{1}{2}$-inch rounds
1 dozen small white mushroom caps, rinsed, sliced
1 small red onion, sliced thin
2 carrots, pared and shredded into twirls
3-4 garlic cloves, minced
Asian Dressing (see page 176)

In a medium-size tray with an edge, arrange the vegetables in decorative sections. In one section lay asparagus; then, a portion of endive rounds; mushrooms; spirals of red onion; a mound of carrot twirls. Sprinkle garlic over dish. Prepare Asian Dressing and sprinkle over tray just before serving. Serves 4. You may wish to present this dish when serving the chicken.

……………………………..

TERIYAKI CHICKEN

4-6 chicken breast halves, boned, skinned, cut into strips, washed, patted dry with
   paper towels

MARINADE:
¼ cup soy sauce
2 tbsp. dry white wine (or rice wine)
2 garlic cloves, minced
1 tbsp. granulated sugar
¼ tsp. ground ginger
2 tbsp. fresh parsley, chopped
2-3 tbsp. peanut oil

Heat oil in a large wok or skillet. Blend soy sauce, wine, garlic, sugar, ginger and
parsley. Brush the marinade on the chicken strips and cook them in the wok on medium-
high heat, stirring and turning them frequently, until chicken is cooked. Transfer to
serving platter to complement vegetables. Serves 4-5.

....

FRESH FRUITS IN GINGER SAUCE

1 pineapple, cored, pared, cut into   2 tbsp. sugar
   chunks   1 cup orange juice
2 cups cantaloupe chunks   1 tbsp. lemon juice
1 cup green seedless grapes   2 tbsp. rum
1 cup strawberries, sliced   1 tbsp. candied ginger

In a medium-size fruit bowl, combine chunks of pineapple, melon, and grapes. In a small
sauce pot, mix juices with sugar. Bring to a boil; lower heat and simmer for 10 minutes.
Remove from heat, stir in rum and ginger. Cool. Add the sauce to the pineapple mix.
Toss and chill. Add the sliced strawberries to the mix just before serving.
Serves 4-6.

❀❀❀❀❀❀❀❀❀❀

Spring Soup
Eggs, Shrimp and Scallops Salad
Macaroon Ambrosia

❀❀❀❀❀❀❀❀❀❀

SPRING SOUP

3 onions, sliced thin
2 stalks celery, cleaned, chopped
2 carrots, pared, sliced thin into rounds
2-4 small Red Bliss potatoes, scrubbed, cut into chunks (with skin)
1 cup shelled peas (or 1 small, 6 oz. can baby peas)
1 cup baby spinach, rinsed, drained
4 cups chicken stock (use canned consommé or mash 4 chicken bouillon cubes
     in 4 cups water)
2 egg yolks or $\frac{1}{2}$ cup egg substitute
1 tsp. salt
$\frac{1}{4}$ tsp. black pepper
$\frac{1}{4}$ cup fresh parsley, chopped
$\frac{1}{4}$ pint light cream or fat-free evaporated milk
2 tbsp. flour
2 tbsp. olive oil

In a 4-quart soup pot with lid, heat oil at medium temperature. Stir in flour. Add and
stir in chicken stock. Add potatoes, celery, onion, carrots and simmer, covered for
20 minutes. Add peas and simmer for another 5 minutes. Add parsley, salt and pepper.
Beat egg with cream and blend into soup, stirring constantly as the soup simmers, for
another 5 minutes. Stir in baby spinach; simmer 2-3 minutes. Turn off heat. Add more
salt and pepper to taste. Serve hot. Serves 4-6.

………………………………..

EGGS, SHRIMP AND SCALLOPS SALAD

4-6 hard boiled eggs, shelled
2 tbsp. olive oil
1 tbsp. wine vinegar
2 cups medium-size shrimp, peeled,
    cleaned
2 cups bay scallops, rinsed, drained
1 large red tomato, sliced in $\frac{1}{4}$-inch
    rounds
1 large yellow tomato, sliced in $\frac{1}{4}$-inch
    rounds
4 Kirbys, scrubbed, scraped, trimmed,
    quartered lengthwise
1 large red onion, sliced thin
$\frac{1}{2}$ cup oil-cured olives, pitted
1 carrot, pared and shredded
4-6 large leaves Boston lettuce
1 small tin, rolled anchovy with capers

SAUCE:
1 cup mayonnaise
$\frac{1}{4}$ cup Honey Mustard Dressing
    (see page 173)
$\frac{1}{4}$ cup lemon juice
Hungarian paprika
$\frac{1}{4}$ cup chives, chopped

Hard cook the eggs; cool in cold water. Simmer scallops and shrimp in a small pot; drain and place in a small bowl with vinegar and oil, stirring the seafood to coat thoroughly. Prepare Honey Mustard Dressing and the sauce by blending mayonnaise, Honey Mustard Dressing and lemon juice in a small bowl. Set aside.

On a large platter, arrange the salad by laying a bed of lettuce leaves over the plate. Next, slice red and yellow tomatoes and arrange them on top of the lettuce. Spread onion slices over tomatoes. Shell the eggs; carefully halve the eggs and place them around the salad platter. Spoon the seafood around the platter. Garnish with Kirby spears. Press the rolled anchovies into the egg halves. Sprinkle with olives. Drizzle the sauce over the salad platter and sprinkle with chives and paprika. Serves 4-6. Italian whole wheat bread, sliced thin, makes a nice accompaniment.

…………………………..

MACAROON AMBROSIA

¼ lb. butter or Smart Balance spread
1 cup granulated sugar
½ cup coconut flakes
½ cup quick oats
2 tbsp. flour
1 egg or ¼ cup egg substitute, beaten
½ tsp. salt
¼ tsp. baking powder
½ tsp. vanilla

1 pt. heavy whipping cream
½ cup chopped, pitted dates
1 doz. fresh cherries with stems

Preheat oven to 350° F. Mix all ingredients together, except whipping cream, dates and cherries. Spread batter on greased pan, 9x13. Bake at 350° F for 20 minutes, until golden brown and darkening around the edges. Remove from the oven and cut immediately into 4x4-inch pieces. Place on cutting board to cool. Cool until hard. Break into small pieces. Whip cream to form stiff peaks. Fold macaroon pieces into whipped cream. Fold in chopped dates. Pour this mix into a large serving bowl. Add the cherries with stems, for a tasty and colorful garnish. Assemble dessert just before serving because the broken macaroons will soften. Serves 6-8.

❁ ❁ ❁ ❁ ❁ ❁ ❁ ❁ ❁ ❁

Mixed Greens with Tarragon
Jambalaya with Seafood
Coffee Sorbet

✿✿✿✿✿✿✿✿✿✿

MIXED GREENS WITH TARRAGON
(Prepare dressing in advance.)

1 cup escarole, rinsed, drained, cut into
    bite-size pieces (use center
    of greens)
1 cup arugula, rinsed, drained, trimmed
2 cups baby spinach, rinsed, drained
1 small red onion, sliced thin
2 tbsp. fresh tarragon leaves, minced
2 garlic cloves, minced

TARRAGON DRESSING:
$\frac{1}{2}$ cup olive oil
2 tbsp. tarragon wine vinegar
1 tbsp. Dijon mustard
$\frac{1}{4}$ tsp. black pepper

Prepare dressing; mix all ingredients in a small jar. Shake well. At serving time pour over greens and toss to mix. Combine escarole, arugula, spinach, onion, garlic and tarragon leaves in a salad bowl. Refrigerate until serving. Proceed as directed. Serves 4-5.

....

JAMBALAYA WITH SEAFOOD

4 tbsp. olive oil
3 garlic cloves chopped
1 large onion, sliced thin
1 cup tomato purée
1 cup canned plum tomatoes, mashed with fork
1 sweet pimiento pepper, chopped
1 small cayenne pepper (add small to medium amount of pepper for desired spiciness; wear protective gloves)
6 small mushrooms, rinsed
1 tsp. salt
1 tsp. sugar
$\frac{1}{2}$ tsp. black pepper
$\frac{1}{2}$ cup dry white wine
2 bay leaves
1 tbsp. dried oregano
2-3 leaves fresh basil, torn
3 cups mixed; large shrimps, cleaned, and sea scallops
1 cup baby squid, cleaned, sliced into thin rounds; include tentacles

In a large flame/heat resistant casserole dish (with a lid), lightly brown onion and garlic in olive oil. Stir in tomato purée and mashed plum tomatoes, peppers and mushrooms. Stir in salt, pepper, sugar, oregano and basil. Simmer for 25 minutes. Stir in all of the seafood; lay 2 bay leaves on top of casserole and cover. Simmer for another 8-10 minutes, or until shrimp are opaque. Stir in wine and remove casserole from heat. Serve over white rice. Serves 4-6.

…………………………..

COFFEE SORBET
(Prepare the day before, up to and including freezing.)

Prepare coffee for 8 people; while hot, stir in 4 tablespoons superfine granulated sugar and $\frac{1}{4}$ cup amaretto liqueur. Cool. Pour into 2 ice trays and leave to freeze for several hours. Remove from freezer 5 minutes before serving. Spoon into stemmed glasses ($\frac{1}{2}$-pt. size). Drizzle 1 teaspoon amaretto over sorbet. Serves 4-6.

❀❀❀❀❀❀❀❀❀❀

Provolone Soup
Chicken and Walnut Salad
Fresh Corn-on-the-Cob
Melon with Pineapple

✿ ✿ ✿ ✿ ✿ ✿ ✿ ✿ ✿ ✿

PROVOLONE SOUP
(Prepare a day or two in advance.)

2 cups chicken stock (use stock from preparation of Chicken and Walnut Salad or
    mash 2 chicken bouillon cubes in 2 cups boiling water)
2 cups milk or evaporated milk
2 tbsp. olive oil
1 cup chopped onion
1 cup chopped celery
2 tbsp. flour
½ tsp. salt
¼ tsp. black pepper
2 cups all-purpose potatoes, peeled, diced, cooked
½ cup fresh or frozen peas
2 ½ cups sharp provolone cheese, shredded
2 slices bacon, cooked crisp, crumbled

Cook bacon and drain on paper towels. Simmer potatoes in small saucepan; set aside.
In soup pot, lightly brown onion and celery in olive oil. Stir in salt and pepper and flour.
Gradually stir in milk, stock, cooked potatoes and peas. Cook the soup over medium
heat, stirring frequently, until it simmers. Remove from heat and stir in cheese. Return
to burner, simmer gently until cheese melts. Stir constantly. Do not allow pot to boil.
Garnish with crumbled bacon. Makes 4-5 servings.

……………………………..

4 halves chicken breasts, skinned, boned, simmered in 2 cups water. Remove cooked
  chicken to cutting board. Save stock for Provolone Soup.
2 eggs, hardboiled, shelled, diced
$\frac{1}{2}$ red pepper, diced
$\frac{1}{2}$ green pepper, diced
2 stalks celery, cleaned, chopped
1 small onion, chopped
2 tbsp. prepared pickle relish
$\frac{1}{2}$ apple, cubed
1 tsp. salt
$\frac{1}{4}$ tsp. black pepper
1 cup Miracle Whip
$\frac{1}{4}$ cup lemon juice
$\frac{1}{2}$ cup chopped walnuts
$\frac{1}{4}$ cup green Sicilian olives, pitted, chopped for garnish
2-3 cups baby spinach, rinsed, drained

Cut the cooked chicken breasts in small chunks. Place chicken in large mixing bowl.
Add all of the ingredients except spinach and olives. Gently mix the chicken salad-don't
mash. Set beds of spinach on 4-5 salad plates. Equally spoon chicken salad onto each
bed of spinach. Garnish with chopped olives. Serves 4-5. Chill until ready to serve.

……………………………..

FRESH CORN-ON-THE-COB goes well as an accompaniment. Include fresh butter or
Smart Balance spread when serving.

……………………………..

MELON WITH PINEAPPLE

1 cantaloupe or honeydew melon
1 small pineapple, cored, rind removed, cut into round $\frac{1}{2}$-inch slices
$\frac{1}{4}$ cup light rum
sprigs of mint for garnish

Wash melon skin and pat dry with paper towel. Place whole melon on cutting board.
With a long sharp knife, cut off both ends of the melon. Slice melon into 1-inch rounds.
Gently cut away the rind from each slice and lay one round slice of melon on each of
4-5 flat salad plates. Lay a trimmed round slice of pineapple on top of each slice of
melon. Drizzle rum over fruit. Chill until serving. Garnish with sprigs of mint.
Serves 4-5.

✿✿✿✿✿✿✿✿✿✿

Oyster Stew
Marinated Corn and Bean Salad
Crab Cakes
Whipped Cream with Berries

❁ ❁ ❁ ❁ ❁ ❁ ❁ ❁ ❁ ❁

OYSTER STEW

2 dozen shucked oysters (ask fishery to include the container of oyster juice)
2 tbsp. butter
2 tbsp. flour
2 cups evaporated milk
½ cup dry vermouth
½ cup heavy cream
¼ tsp. cayenne pepper
1 tsp. grated nutmeg
1 tbsp. chopped parsley
1 cup liquid from oysters, strained
1 tsp. salt
½ cup chopped celery

Remove sacs from oysters. Rinse oysters in cold water and drain; set in refrigerator until needed. In a 3-quart saucepan with lid, melt butter on low heat; stir in flour. Raise heat and stir in evaporated milk. Simmer for 2-3 minutes. Add chopped celery as you cook. Blend in vermouth, heavy cream, oyster stock, cayenne, nutmeg and salt. Cover and simmer low for 8–10 minutes, stirring often. In last 2-3 minutes, add cleaned whole oysters. Continue to simmer for 1-2 minutes. Serves 4-5. Sprinkle chopped parsley over individual bowls. Oyster crackers go well with this soup.

…………………………..

MARINATED CORN AND BEAN SALAD

1 can (1 lb.) black beans, rinsed in cold water, drained
1 can (1 lb.) ceci, rinsed in cold water, drained
1 can (1 lb.) corn kernels, rinsed in cold water, drained
2 cups fresh green beans, cut in 2-inch pieces, cooked al dente, drained
½ red pepper, chopped
½ green pepper, chopped
2 garlic cloves, chopped
1 small onion, chopped
¼ cup pitted, oil-cured olives
¼ cup apple cider vinegar
¼ cup olive oil
¼ tsp. black pepper
1 tbsp. balsamic vinegar
½ cup fresh blueberries
4-5 large leaves Boston lettuce

Lay 4-5 lettuce leaves on base of a large serving platter. Arrange the corn, beans, ceci and green beans in sections on lettuce. Over corn, garnish with chopped red pepper; over black beans, sprinkle onion; over ceci, garnish with garlic; spread green pepper over green beans. Mix oil, vinegar and pepper in a small cup. Strew blueberries and olives over platter; then, sprinkle the dressing over the salad. Cover with plastic wrap and refrigerate for 1 hour before serving. Serves 4-5.

....

CRAB CAKES
(May be prepared day before and thoroughly warmed before serving.)

2 lbs. crab meat in small chunks
3 egg whites, lightly beaten
¼ cup finely chopped onion
2 tbsp. chopped parsley
2 tsp. dried thyme, crushed
2 tsp. Worcestershire sauce

¼ cup mayonnaise
1 ½ cups unseasoned bread crumbs
½ cup cornmeal
4 tbsp. canola oil
lemon wedges for garnish

In large mixing bowl, combine crabmeat chunks, onion, parsley, thyme, egg whites, Worcestershire sauce, mayonnaise, 1 cup bread crumbs (reserve ½ cup for coating). Blend cornmeal and rest of crumbs and spread on a sheet of waxed paper. Heat canola oil in large skillet. Shape 6-8 crab patties, about 1-inch thick, with your hands. Coat on each side with crumb-cornmeal mix. Fry cakes in oil on medium heat for 3-4 minutes on each side or until golden, and heated through. Add additional oil if necessary. Serve hot with lemon wedges. Serves 4-5.

....

WHIPPED CREAM WITH BERRIES

1 pt. blueberries, rinsed, drained
½ pt. blackberries, gently rinsed and drained
½ pt. raspberries, gently rinsed, drained
1 cup sliced fresh strawberries (trimmed, rinsed, drained, before slicing)
1 pt. heavy whipping cream
¼ cup cherry liqueur
1 dozen or so fresh Bing or Queen Anne cherries, with stems, washed, drained

Beat cream to stiff peaks. Assemble the berries in a large decorative glass bowl.
Blueberries are placed at bottom; spoon a layer of whipped cream; add a layer of
raspberries and more cream; then, lay the blackberries with more cream; finally, add
sliced strawberries; and top with rest of whipped cream. Drizzle the liqueur over bowl
and garnish with stemmed cherries. Spoon into individual bowls when serving.
Serves 4-6.

❀❀❀❀❀❀❀❀❀❀

Escarole and Arugula with Ricotta Salata
Pasta with Salmon
Banana Trifle

❀ ❀ ❀ ❀ ❀ ❀ ❀ ❀ ❀ ❀

ESCAROLE AND ARUGULA WITH RICOTTA SALATA

2 cups arugula, trimmed, washed and drained
3 cups escarole (use center of head), washed and drained
2 large beefsteak tomatoes, cut into rounds; then, halve each slice
½ lb. chunk ricotta salata, crumbled
4-6 basil leaves, torn into pieces
1 tbsp. dried oregano
1 dozen scallions, trimmed, washed
Italian Dressing (see page 173)

Pour the greens into a wide, shallow bowl, for serving. Add basil and oregano and crumbled cheese. Prepare dressing and pour over greens. Toss to coat thoroughly. Decorate the edge of the bowl with half- moon slices of tomato. Insert scallions into salad (as straws). Serves 4-6.

…………………………..

PASTA WITH SALMON

8 oz. pasta, bow ties or rotelle
6-8 small mushrooms, rinsed, quartered
1 can (1 lb.) whole artichoke hearts, unseasoned, rinsed, drained, quartered
4-6 garlic cloves, leave whole
1 lg. onion, chopped
6 basil leaves, torn into pieces
1 tsp. dried oregano
½ tsp. coarsely ground black pepper
1 tsp. salt

2 tbsp. olive oil
1 pt. ricotta
½ cup grated Parmesan cheese
1 ½ lbs. wild salmon fillet; cut off skin, roast at 450° F for 15-20 minutes and cut into 2-3-inch chunks (pepper to taste)
olive oil
juice of 1 lemon
¼ cup chopped fresh Italian parsley
Hungarian paprika

Preheat oven to 450° F . Lay skinned salmon fillet in olive oil-coated pan, 9x12. Brush the fillet with more oil and sprinkle black pepper to taste. Squeeze juice of 1 lemon over fish. Roast for 15-18 minutes; cut into chunks in pan and set aside. In a 1-quart saucepan, heat 2 tablespoons olive oil, and lightly sauté onions and garlic cloves; while stirring, add artichokes and mushrooms and stir over medium heat for 2 minutes. Remove pot from heat and set aside. Cook the pasta al dente, as directed on package. Drain in colander and return pasta to large cooking pot. Spoon ricotta and Parmesan into hot pasta and toss to mix. Place pot on warm burner as you add the artichoke and mushroom mix. With a spatula remove salmon chunks to pasta pot and very gently, toss the pasta mix (keep warm). Immediately, transfer the contents into a very large serving platter about 2 inches deep. Sprinkle pasta and salmon with parsley and paprika. Serves 4-6. Delicioso!

…………………………..

BANANA TRIFLE

4 bananas, peeled and sliced lengthways, each into 3-4 slices
½ pint raspberries, gently rinsed and drained
½ pint blackberries, gently rinsed and drained
4 tbsp. raspberry jam with seeds
1 pt. heavy whipping cream, whipped into peaks
4 tbsp. sherry
1 pkg. lady fingers

Ready a 7x9 baking pan (preferably Pyrex) from which you will serve the trifle; line the bottom of the pan with lady fingers, flat side up. Spread with raspberry jam. Spread with raspberries. Sprinkle 2 tablespoons sherry over raspberries. Spread one-half of the whipped cream over berries. Lay the sliced bananas over the cream. Spread with blackberries. Sprinkle rest of sherry over blackberries; spread rest of whipped cream over blackberries. Leave to rest in refrigerator for 1 hour before serving. Use spatulas to slice and serve onto dessert dishes. Serves 4-5.

❀❀❀❀❀❀❀❀❀❀

Chicken Fingers Salad OR (Roasted Salmon Salad)
Curried Wild Rice and Cranberries
Melon Bowl Crunch

❀❀❀❀❀❀❀❀❀❀❀

CHICKEN FINGERS SALAD (OR: ROASTED SALMON SALAD)

4-5 chicken breasts, halved, boned, skinned, washed, drained, cut 1-in. strips OR
1 ½ lbs. salmon fillet (remove skin), cut into small chunks
1 cup flour: mix 1 tsp. black pepper into flour and pour onto a sheet of waxed paper and
    1 cup corn flake crumbs: pour onto a sheet of waxed paper (for chicken ONLY)
½ cup olive oil
⅛ cup balsamic vinegar
oil to coat pan

SALAD:
6 cups greens: green leaf lettuce, red leaf lettuce, baby spinach, romaine, radicchio
1 red pepper, cored, sliced into thin strips
4-6 white mushrooms, rinsed, sliced thin
4-6 plum tomatoes, trimmed, sliced into rounds
2 cups shredded carrots
1 lb. can ceci, rinsed, drained
3-4 garlic cloves, chopped
1 small red onion, sliced thin
1 cup blueberries or red grapes (or 1 cup pitted calamata olives for a smoky taste)
1 dozen small mozzarella balls (in water), drained
Parmesan Cheese Dressing (see page 176)

Pour oil and balsamic vinegar in a small bowl. Have ready: 2 sheets of waxed paper; one
sheet with flour and black pepper mix and the other sheet with corn flake crumbs. Oil
bottom of baking tin, 9x13. Preheat oven to 450° F. Brush each strip of chicken with oil
mix; coat with flour mix; brush again with oil mix and coat with corn flake crumbs. Lay
strips, side-by-side in 9x13-inch prepared pan. Roast in oven, 450° F for 7-10 minutes on
each side, until lightly browned. (Or: baste salmon with oil and balsamic vinegar; roast
at 400° F, 25 minutes.)

As the chicken (or salmon) roasts, prepare the salad. Into a very large, shallow serving
dish, combine bite-size greens, onions, garlic, red pepper, mushrooms, ceci , fruit (OR
olives), and mozzarella balls. Prepare Parmesan Dressing and pour over salad; toss to
mix. When chicken is cooked, remove crusty strips from pan and lay them over the salad.
(Substitute: small chunks roasted salmon.) Serve immediately with a side of Curried Rice
and crusty artisan bread (or pecan-raisin bread or olive bread). Serves 4-6 generously.

………………………………..

CURRIED WILD RICE AND CRANBERRIES

2 cups cooked rice (a mixture of white and wild rice: prepare by simmering, covered,
 $\frac{1}{2}$ cup white rice, $\frac{1}{2}$ cup pre-soaked wild rice into 2 cups boiling water for
 25 minutes.)
$\frac{1}{2}$ cup mayonnaise
$\frac{1}{4}$ cup olive oil
2 tbsp. wine vinegar
2 garlic cloves, minced
$\frac{1}{2}$ tsp. curry powder
$\frac{1}{2}$ cup dried cranberries
$\frac{1}{2}$ cup dry vermouth
$\frac{1}{2}$ cup pignola (pine nuts)

In a small bowl, blend mayonnaise, oil, vinegar, garlic and curry. Set aside. In a small
bowl combine dried cranberries and vermouth. Allow to sit for 10 minutes. After rice is
steamed, while still quite warm, stir in cranberries mix. In a small skillet coated with a
scant teaspoon of olive oil, lightly brown the pine nuts. Add them to the rice mix and
pour the mayonnaise dressing mix into the rice mix. Toss gently with 2 spoons. (This is a
recipe to fill a colorful crock which resembles half a squash or pumpkin.) Serve at room
temperature. Serves 4-6, to accompany the chicken salad.

……………………………..

MELON BOWL CRUNCH

2-3 small cantaloupes, halved, seeds removed
2-3 pts. vanilla yogurt
4 tbsp. quick-cooking oats
$\frac{1}{4}$ cup chopped walnuts
$\frac{1}{2}$ cup each: raspberries, blueberries

Place cantaloupe halves on paper doily-covered dessert plates. In a mixing bowl, spoon
yogurt. Add oats, nuts and berries and gently fold into yogurt. Spoon mix into melon
cavities and serve. Serves 4-6.

Caponata
Salmon Croquettes and Asparagus
Coupe Saint-André

❁ ❁ ❁ ❁ ❁ ❁ ❁ ❁ ❁ ❁ ❁

CAPONATA
(Prepare a day in advance.)

2 medium-size eggplant (do not pare); cut eggplant lengthwise into $\frac{1}{2}$-inch slices; lay on waxed paper and sprinkle both sides of each slice with salt. Allow the slices to sit for 15 minutes to rid the eggplant of excess moisture. Wash the salt off with cold water; squeeze 2-3 slices together, between your hands, rinse in cold water and pat dry with paper towels. In a large skillet with a lid, cover bottom with $\frac{1}{4}$ cup olive oil and sauté the slices over high heat until brown. Turn frequently. Remove to board. Cut each slice into 1-inch strips vertically; then, cut into 1-inch cubes horizontally. Set aside.

1 cup chopped onions, 2-3 small
$\frac{1}{2}$ cup chopped celery
2 garlic cloves, chopped
$\frac{1}{2}$ cup Greek olives, pitted
$\frac{1}{2}$ cup Sicilian olives, pitted
$\frac{1}{2}$ cup red pepper, chopped
2 tbsp. capers
3 tbsp. tomato paste
2 tsp. brown sugar
2 tbsp. balsamic vinegar
$\frac{1}{2}$ tsp. black pepper
$\frac{1}{4}$ tsp. cayenne pepper
1 tsp. dried oregano
$\frac{1}{2}$ tsp. dried thyme
1 tsp. chopped fresh basil
2 tbsp. Marsala or Madeira wine
red leaf lettuce (for salad bowls), wash and drain

After the eggplant is cooked and cubed and set aside on a board, turn heat in skillet to low; add a little more olive oil, if necessary and simmer onions until opaque. Stir in celery and garlic; simmer for 2-3 minutes; add tomato paste and stir on low heat for 5 minutes longer. Add eggplant and the rest of ingredients (herbs, spices, sugar); except wine. Simmer, covered for 10-12 minutes; stir occasionally. Remove from heat and stir in sweet wine; allow to cool. Refrigerate. At serving time, line small salad bowls with red leaf lettuce and spoon caponata into bowls. Serve with crusty Italian bread. Serves 4-6.

....

SALMON CROQUETTES AND ASPARAGUS
(Prepare croquettes day before.)

1 $\frac{1}{2}$ lbs. salmon fillets, remove skin, steam in pan with lid, water to cover for 5 minutes;
    drain well; set aside
2 eggs or ($\frac{1}{2}$ cup egg substitute)
$\frac{1}{2}$ cup unseasoned bread crumbs
3-4 medium, boiled, pared potatoes, mashed
$\frac{1}{2}$ cup minced onion
$\frac{1}{2}$ cup minced celery
$\frac{1}{4}$ tsp. black pepper, salt to taste
$\frac{1}{4}$ cup chopped fresh parsley
canola oil for frying, about 4 tbsp.
1 cup flour for coating

In a large mixing bowl, beat eggs; flake the cooked salmon and add to bowl. Add mashed potatoes, onion, celery, pepper, salt, parsley and crumbs. Blend to mix well. Form croquettes with a large serving spoon and your hands; coat in flour on all sides. Fry in preheated skillet with canola oil (320° F). Turn 2-3 times; cook until light brown. Remove to paper towels; then to heat-proof serving platter. Cover lightly with foil; refrigerate. Heat thoroughly in oven, 275° F before serving. Steamed asparagus make a nice accompaniment. Serve 4-5 asparagus spears for each portion. Croquettes serve 4-5.

…………………………..

COUPE SAINT-ANDRÉ

2 cups strawberries, washed, drained, sliced
$\frac{1}{2}$ pt. raspberries, gently rinsed and drained
1 cup fresh peaches with skin, sliced
2-3 apricots, quartered
4-6 tbsp. strawberry or cherry liqueur
strawberry ice cream
1 pt. heavy whipping cream

Mix all of the fruit in a large bowl. Refrigerate until serving. Beat cream into stiff peaks. Serve in frappe dessert glasses. Spoon fruit into glasses, up to 2 inches to rim. Moisten fruit with liqueur. Add one scoop of strawberry ice cream on top of fruit. Garnish with whipped cream. Serve with iced tea spoons. Serves 4-6.

❁❁❁❁❁❁❁❁❁❁❁

Chicken and Vegetable Soup
Mexican Scallops Salad
Pineapple Sundae

❀ ❀ ❀ ❀ ❀ ❀ ❀ ❀ ❀ ❀ ❀

CHICKEN AND VEGETABLE SOUP
(Prepare on day before.)

2 tbsp. olive oil
1 large onion, chopped
3 garlic cloves, chopped
4 tbsp. flour
2 cups water
4 cups chicken stock
1 large carrot, chopped
1 pkg. (1 lb.) frozen baby lima beans
$\frac{1}{2}$ cup fresh green beans, trimmed, cut into small pieces
1 cup canned corn kernels, drained
1 tsp. each: salt, dried oregano, dried basil
$\frac{1}{2}$ tsp. cayenne pepper
$\frac{1}{4}$ tsp. black pepper
1 small cayenne pepper-chopped, optional (wear plastic gloves)
1 full breast (2 pieces) chicken, boned, skinned

Prepare chicken stock by simmering chicken breast in 4 cups water, until cooked. Remove chicken to board and cut into bite-size pieces; set aside. In a large saucepan, heat oil and brown onion and garlic. Stir in flour and cook for 1-2 minutes stirring to blend. Add water and stock, scraping bottom of pot to mix. Stir and cook for 2 minutes at high heat until smooth. Add vegetables, spices and chicken. Bring to a boil; reduce heat to medium-low; cover and simmer for 30 minutes until vegetables are tender. Adjust spices to suit taste. Serves 6.

. . . .

MEXICAN SCALLOPS SALAD

4 tbsp. olive oil
2 lbs. sea scallops, washed, drained
4 scallions, sliced thin
4 garlic cloves, minced
1-2 chile peppers, seeded, chopped (wear plastic gloves)
2 tbsp. fresh cilantro, chopped
juice of 1 lime
1 tsp. salt
¼ tsp. black pepper
green leaf lettuce leaves, rinsed, drained
red bell pepper, seeded, sliced thin
calamata olives (about 4-6 per serving)
Aioli Sauce (see page 177)

Heat oil in heavy skillet. At medium-high heat, sauté scallops; cook quickly, until just opaque, turning scallops frequently. Remove to warm platter. Add scallions and garlic to skillet and cook for a couple of minutes until scallions start to wilt. Return scallops to pan. Add chiles, cilantro, salt, pepper and lime juice. Stir to mix. Have serving platter ready with a bed of lettuce, sliced red pepper and olives. With a spatula, remove scallops mix from skillet onto salad bed. Serve immediately. Serves 4-6.

....

PINEAPPLE SUNDAE

1 fresh pineapple; slice off top and bottom. With large knife, cut into horizontal slices, 1-inch thick. Cut away rind. Lay one slice of pineapple on each dessert dish. Sprinkle with brown sugar. Add a ball of vanilla ice cream in center of each pineapple ring. Sprinkle with Grand Marnier (or an orange liqueur), 1 teaspoon per serving. Serves 4-6.

✿✿✿✿✿✿✿✿✿✿✿

Red Snapper Modena
Latin Grill Salad
Cantaloupe with Brandied Cherries

❀ ❀ ❀ ❀ ❀ ❀ ❀ ❀ ❀ ❀

RED SNAPPER MODENA

4 fillets red snapper, skin removed
1 cup cracker meal
black pepper, salt to taste
¼ cup fresh cilantro, chopped
Hungarian paprika
2 eggs beaten or ½ cup egg substitute

olive oil for non-stick pan 9x13
4 tbsp. balsamic vinegar
4 cups baby spinach, rinsed, drained
1 small red onion, thinly sliced
2 tbsp. olive oil, 4 tbsp. balsamic vinegar
   for sprinkling

Beat eggs in a shallow bowl. Preheat oven to 375° F and lightly coat 9x13 non-stick pan with olive oil. Pour cracker meal mixed with salt, pepper and cilantro onto a sheet of waxed paper. Coat bottom of pan with olive oil. Dip each fillet in beaten egg; coat with cracker meal mix. Lay side by side in pan. Sprinkle 1 tablespoon balsamic vinegar and paprika over each fillet. Bake in oven 375° F for 25 minutes or until lightly browned. Do not overcook. Remove gently with a spatula to individual plates which you've prepared with a cupful of raw spinach and slices of onion. Sprinkle more olive oil and balsamic vinegar over spinach mix and lay a fillet on top. Serves 4.

………………………………..

LATIN GRILL SALAD
(Prepare salsa day before.)

4 small eggplants, cut off stem and bottom; peel, cut in half, lengthwise (if thicker than
   2 inches in diameter, slice each into 3 parts)
4 slender zucchini, cut off stem and bottom, scrape skin, but do not pare; cut lengthwise
   in 2-3 slices
¼ cup olive oil
2 tbsp. balsamic vinegar

Set grill or broiler on high. Brush both sides of each slice of eggplant and zucchini. Grill 2-3 minutes on each side. Remove to platter. Spoon salsa over each serving of vegetables as they are served. (See recipe for SALSA, next page.)

SALSA:

1 small can (6 oz.) each: black beans, red kidney beans, corn kernels
½ cup chopped pitted spicy olives
1 cup chopped plum tomatoes, with skin
1 small onion, chopped
2 garlic cloves, minced
2 tbsp. olive oil
1 tbsp. balsamic vinegar
1 tbsp. dried oregano
1 tsp. salt
1 tsp. cayenne pepper
1 small chile, chopped (to taste); use plastic gloves when handling
1 bay leaf

In a small bowl, mix all Salsa ingredients and top with bay leaf. Seal with plastic wrap and refrigerate until needed. Spoon over eggplant and zucchini at serving. Serves 4-5.

………………………………..

CANTALOUPE WITH BRANDIED CHERRIES

1 large (or 2 small) ripe cantaloupe; or 1 honey dew melon and 1 small cantaloupe; wash
    skin thoroughly before handling. Peel the skin off the melons, remove seeds and cut
    them into neat bite-size cubes.
2 cups Bing cherries, pitted
2 oz. brandy
juice of 1 lemon
sprigs of mint

Place pitted cherries into a small bowl; add the brandy; cover and refrigerate for 1 hour.
Prepare melon as directed and place into large glass fruit bowl; cover with plastic and
refrigerate until needed. At serving time, squeeze juice of lemon over the melon and top
with brandied cherries. Garnish with mint. Serves 4-6, generously.

❀❀❀❀❀❀❀❀❀❀

Cobb Salad with Beets and Onions
Tuscan Pasta and Shrimp
Coupe Saint-Jacques

❀ ❀ ❀ ❀ ❀ ❀ ❀ ❀ ❀ ❀ ❀

COBB SALAD WITH BEETS AND ONIONS

3 cups romaine lettuce, rinsed, drained, shredded vertically
1 jar (1 lb.) pickled beets, drained
1 cup diced, cured ham
1 small red onion, sliced thin
1 hard-cooked egg, chopped
Vinaigrette Dressing (see page 177)

Prepare individual serving plates. Arrange romaine lettuce on bottom of plate. In the center, add beets, ham and onion. Sprinkle chopped egg over each dish. Drizzle dressing on salad just before serving. Serves 4-5.

……………………………..

TUSCAN PASTA AND SHRIMP

8 oz. whole wheat rotelle pasta
1 lb. small shrimp, cleaned, simmered for 2 minutes, (unless precooked), drained
1 cup cherry or grape tomatoes, halved
$\frac{1}{4}$ cup fresh basil, torn
$\frac{1}{2}$ tsp. each: dried rosemary, oregano
bay leaf
salt and pepper to taste
2 tbsp. olive oil
$\frac{1}{2}$ cup grated Asiago cheese
Parmesan Cheese Dressing, see page 176
6 oz. baby spinach, rinsed, drained thoroughly

Lay a bed of spinach on each pasta serving dish. Cook pasta al dente in a large pot as directed on package. Drain in colander, rinse with cold water and drain again. Pour pasta into a large colorful mixing bowl and toss with olive oil. Add and combine cooked shrimp, tomato halves, basil, salt, pepper and herbs. Sprinkle with Asiago cheese. Drizzle with Parmesan Dressing at serving time and toss to mix. Spoon onto beds of spinach. Serves 4-6.

……………………………..

COUPE SAINT-JACQUES

3-4 Bartlett pears, cored, sliced vertically into $\frac{1}{2}$-inch lengths (do not remove skin)
lemon sherbet
1 cup red seedless grapes, rinsed, drained
$\frac{1}{2}$ pt. raspberries, gently rinsed, drained
chocolate fudge sauce, 1 tbsp. per serving
(tall ice cream parlor glasses will dress up this dessert)

Line each glass with spears of pears, skin showing through outside of glass. Scoop sherbet into center of glasses. Add grapes and raspberries and drizzle chocolate sauce on top. Serves 4-5.

❁❁❁❁❁❁❁❁❁❁

Tomato, Mozzarella and Figs
Chicken, Pasta and Artichokes
Stuffed Peaches

✿✿✿✿✿✿✿✿✿✿

TOMATO, MOZZARELLA AND FIGS

2 large beefsteak tomatoes, chilled in refrigerator
1 lb. mozzarella or 1 $\frac{1}{2}$ dozen tiny mozzarella balls
4-6 fresh figs: Black Turkey, Kadota, Calimyrna
$\frac{1}{2}$ pt. fresh blackberries, gently rinsed and drained
1 dozen basil leaves, rinsed and drained
$\frac{1}{4}$ cup virgin olive oil
salt, black pepper to taste
1 tbsp. dried oregano, 2-3 garlic cloves, chopped

Slice the tomatoes into one-half inch rounds. Arrange them on a large, flat, glass plate. Thinly slice mozzarella and lay the pieces on the tomatoes. (Or strew mozzarella balls over the tomatoes.) Tuck basil leaves between cheese and tomato slices. Cut off stems on figs. Quarter the figs and arrange the pieces around the platter. Scatter garlic over the salad; scatter the berries over the salad. Sprinkle with oregano, salt and pepper and drizzle olive oil over plate. Serve with crusty Italian bread. Serves 4-5.

....

CHICKEN, PASTA AND ARTICHOKES

8 oz. cut ziti, cooked al dente or as
    directed on package and drained.
    Rinse in cool water and drain again.
    Pour in large serving bowl; add 2-3
    tablespoons olive oil and toss;
    set aside.
3 chicken breast halves, boned, skinned,
    cooked in 1 cup water, drained and
    cut into chunks; save stock
3-4 links chicken sausages, grilled,
    sliced into 1-inch rounds
3-4 white mushrooms, rinsed, sliced
1 can (1 lb.) unseasoned artichoke
    hearts, drained, quartered

1 small can (4 oz.) sliced water
    chestnuts, drained
4-6 scallions, trimmed (leave tops),
    chopped
1 cup mayonnaise
$\frac{1}{2}$ cup stock from chicken
1 tbsp. chopped fresh cilantro
1 tsp. curry powder
1 tsp. salt
$\frac{1}{4}$ tsp. black pepper
$\frac{1}{2}$ tsp. cumin
2 tbsp. lemon juice
Hungarian paprika
romaine lettuce, rinsed, drained

In a large mixing bowl, combine cooked ziti, chicken chunks, cooked sausage rounds, mushrooms, artichokes, water chestnuts and scallions. In a small bowl blend thoroughly: mayonnaise, cilantro, $\frac{1}{2}$ cup stock from chicken, curry, salt, pepper, cumin and lemon juice. Pour over chicken and pasta mix. Mix thoroughly. Prepare serving dishes by forming a large daisy with the romaine on each dish. Spoon a generous serving of chicken, pasta and artichokes into center of lettuce daisy. Sprinkle paprika to garnish. Serves 4-6.

....

STUFFED PEACHES

4-5 large peaches; poach them in boiling water for 2 minutes. Remove, drain, and
    peel off skin
juice of 1 lemon
vanilla ice cream
1 pt. raspberries, gently rinsed, drained
2 tbsp. brandy or cherry liqueur
whipped cream
3-4 tbsp. slivered almonds, for garnish

With a fork, mash raspberries in a small bowl. Sprinkle brandy over berries. Set in refrigerator for 1 hour. Lay a peeled peach-half (or two) in each dessert bowl. Sprinkle lemon juice over peaches to prevent discoloration. Refrigerate. Just before serving, add one scoop of ice cream in center of peaches. Spoon some raspberry sauce over the ice cream. Garnish with whipped cream and sprinkle slivered almonds over the cream. Serves 4-6.

❁❁❁❁❁❁❁❁❁

Niçoise Salad
Zucchini Quiche
Ambrosia Cream

✿✿✿✿✿✿✿✿✿✿

NIÇOISE SALAD

4-5 hard cooked eggs, shelled, sliced
2-3 beefsteak tomatoes, sliced into rounds
2 ripe avocados, skinned, stone removed, sliced in thin wedges
18-20 asparagus spears, trimmed, rinsed, steamed for 2-3 minutes
1 can (8 oz.) tuna fish in chunks, drained
12 sardines in oil
1 red onion, sliced thin
2-3 garlic cloves, chopped
½ cup oil-cured olives, pitted
1-2 carrots, pared, shredded
4 tbsp. red wine vinegar
4 tbsp. olive oil
1 cup grated provolone cheese
salt, pepper to taste
1 bunch green leaf lettuce

This salad is supposed to not only taste good, but also should be good to look at.
You may serve from one large platter or on individual salad plates.

As a base for the platter (or plates) lay a bed of green leaf lettuce. Spread the shredded
carrot in center of platter; put the tuna chunks and sardines on top of carrots. Spread the
grated provolone in a ring over the lettuce, around the fish mix. On the cheese, lay slices
of tomato and slices of onion and slices of avocado; decorate with spears of asparagus.
Sprinkle chopped garlic and olives over the mix. In a small bowl blend oil and wine
vinegar, salt and pepper. Sprinkle over entire platter. Serves 4-6, generously.

....

ZUCCHINI QUICHE

1 cup Bisquick mix
3 cups thin, round slices, unpared zucchini
1 tsp. salt
$\frac{1}{4}$ tsp. black pepper
1 chopped onion
$\frac{1}{2}$ red pepper, chopped
$\frac{1}{2}$ cup spicy pepperoni, sliced in slivers
1 tsp. dried oregano
2 tbsp. chopped fresh parsley
2-3 garlic cloves, minced
2 cups mozzarella, grated
4 eggs or 1 cup egg substitute, beaten
olive oil for pan

Heat oven to 350° F. Grease a 9x13-inch pan. In a large bowl, mix all ingredients. Pour into greased pan. Bake until golden brown and set, about 35 minutes. Test with toothpick. Slice into squares. Serve warm or cool. Serves 4-6.

………………………………..

AMBROSIA CREAM

5 cups sour cream
1 $\frac{1}{2}$ cups granulated sugar
1 tbsp. lemon juice
2 egg whites
1 tbsp. light rum
1 tsp. vanilla
4 tbsp. cold water
1 $\frac{1}{2}$ envelopes gelatin (enough to set 2 $\frac{1}{2}$ cups liquid)
1 pt. heavy cream for whipping

In a large bowl, beat sour cream with sugar until foamy. Beat egg whites in a small bowl until stiff. Fold egg whites into sour cream mix. Fold in lemon juice, rum and vanilla. Soften gelatin in cold water, stirring to dissolve and add to mixture. Whisk to blend mix evenly. Refrigerate several hours until set. Beat the cream just before serving. Remove gelatin bowl from refrigerator; dip bowl for 20-30 seconds in hot water. Have a decorative plate ready. Invert the bowl onto the plate and remove the bowl carefully. Decorate around the edge of and on top of the dessert with whipped cream.
Serve immediately. Serves 6.

❀❀❀❀❀❀❀❀❀❀

Mandarin Orange Salad
Brochette of Scallops with Rice
Lemon Ice

❀ ❀ ❀ ❀ ❀ ❀ ❀ ❀ ❀ ❀

MANDARIN ORANGE SALAD

2 cups red leaf lettuce, torn, rinsed, drained
2 cups baby spinach, rinsed, drained
½ cup chopped walnuts
1 cup chopped celery
1 small red onion, sliced thin
1 can (6 oz.) mandarin oranges, drained
Caesar Dressing (see page 175)

Combine all ingredients in large bowl. Chill. Prepare Caesar Dressing and pour on salad just before serving. Toss and mix thoroughly. Serves 4-5.

....

BROCHETTE OF SCALLOPS WITH RICE

2 ½ lbs. sea scallops, rinsed, drained
½ cup dry white wine
1 small onion, minced
2 tbsp. chopped parsley
2 tbsp. white wine vinegar
½ tsp. salt
¼ tsp. black pepper

1 tbsp. lemon juice
2 tbsp. olive oil
12 or more slices of bacon
1 dozen small baby bella mushrooms, rinsed
2-3 red peppers, cored, quartered
4-6 long metal skewers

Heat grill (or broiler) to hot temperature, 475° F. Prepare the marinade. In a small bowl, blend dry wine, onion, parsley, salt, pepper, lemon juice, white wine vinegar and oil. Reserve half of the mix and pour the other half over the scallops in a large bowl and stir to mix. Cut each strip of bacon in half (one half-piece for each scallop). Prepare the baby bellas and red peppers as directed. Arrange each brochette as follows: red pepper, wrapped scallop, mushroom, wrapped scallop, mushroom, 2 wrapped scallops, red pepper. Wrap each scallop in one-half slice of bacon as you skewer the mix. Brush each brochette with reserved marinade. Lay a double sheet of foil on grill; if broiling, use a metal tray. Grill at hot temperature, turning brochettes frequently for about 12-15 minutes. Scallops will start to brown. Serve on a platter with saffron rice. Serves 4-6.

....

SAFFRON RICE

1 cup long grain rice
2 cups chicken broth (less-salt)
¼ tsp. black pepper
1 tbsp. fresh chopped parsley
½ green pepper, chopped
1 small onion, chopped
½-1 tsp. saffron threads

Mix all ingredients in a saucepan; cover and bring to a boil. Lower heat and simmer for 20-25 minutes. Serve a large spoonful of rice with each brochette of scallops.

………………………………..

LEMON ICE

2 cans (11 oz. each) concentrated lemonade
OR 1 can lemonade, 1 can limeade
4 cups crushed ice (use ice crusher, set at "fine")

Soften concentrated lemonade. Pour softened lemonade into a 2-quart pitcher. Add 4 cups, finely crushed ice to pitcher. Stir quickly to blend. Spoon into tall glasses and serve immediately. Serves 4-6.

✿✿✿✿✿✿✿✿✿✿

SUMMER–FALL

SUMMER–FALL

Avocado Salad
Tipsy Pork
Bean Stew
Fruit Almandine

✿✿✿✿✿✿✿✿✿✿

AVOCADO SALAD

1 large avocado or 2 medium, pared, mashed, discard stone
2 small onions, chopped
2 tomatoes, peeled by resting tomatoes in boiling water for 2 minutes, chopped
1 small chile (spicy) or Italian fryer, chopped
1 tsp. salt
$\frac{1}{4}$ tsp. black pepper
1 tsp. Hungarian paprika
4-5 large leaves Boston lettuce
French Dressing (see page 174)

In a 2–quart mixing bowl, blend mashed avocado, chopped onions, tomatoes, chile pepper, salt and black pepper. Cover with plastic and refrigerate. Serve on individual salad plates lined with lettuce. Drizzle French Dressing over the salsa. Tortilla chips make a nice accompaniment. Serves 4-5.

....

TIPSY PORK

4-6 loin pork chops, boneless, trimmed
4-6 garlic cloves, peeled, chop 1 clove
2 fennel bulbs, trimmed, washed, finely
    sliced vertically

4 tsp. capers (juniper berries)
2 tbsp. olive oil
1 cup red wine
salt, black pepper to taste

Preheat grill on broiler to high 450–475° F. In a small bowl mix 1 clove chopped garlic, olive oil, wine, salt, pepper and capers. Make a small slit and place 1 clove of garlic in center of each chop. Brush chops on both sides with marinade. Lay them on a metal tray. Reserve rest of marinade for when you broil the chops. Lay some fennel slices on top of each chop. Refrigerate, covered with plastic for 1 hour. Grill or broil at high temperature, 5 inches away from heat for 15-20 minutes, turning chops over once or twice. Baste with marinade. Do not overcook. Chops are cooked when meat thermometer registers 185° F. Serves 4-5.

....

BEAN STEW

1 can (1 lb.) red kidney beans	2 tbsp. chopped red onion
1 can (1 lb.) corn kernels	2 tbsp. olive oil
1 can (1 lb.) black beans	2 tbsp. red wine vinegar
½ red pepper, chopped	½ tsp. salt
½ green pepper, chopped	¼ tsp. black pepper
2 garlic cloves, minced	

Mix all ingredients in bowl. Pour into 9x12 heat- resistant serving casserole dish. Lay a piece of foil over dish and warm in preheated oven 275° F for 20 minutes; serves 4-5, warm, or at room temperature.

…………………………..

FRUIT ALMANDINE

Fresh fruits are preferred. Select 4-5.

5 cups fruit: pineapple chunks, apricot quarters, sliced pears, pitted cherries, grapes, sliced bananas
2 slices plain pound cake, toasted lightly, crumbled
½ cup sherry
½ cup almonds, slivered, toasted; lay nuts on foil and brown slightly, stirring often, in preheated oven, 475° F for 2 minutes

Toast pound cake lightly, crumble. Set aside. Mix all fruits in sherry in a large serving bowl. Sprinkle with crumbled cake and toasted almonds. Serves 4-6.

✿✿✿✿✿✿✿✿✿✿

Cannellini Bean Salad
Stuffed Red Snapper and Stir-Fry Noodles
Coffee Marshmallow Cream

✧ ✧ ✧ ✧ ✧ ✧ ✧ ✧ ✧ ✧

CANNELLINI BEAN SALAD

1 can (1 lb.) cannellini beans, rinsed, drained	1 tbsp. Italian parsley, chopped
1 small onion, chopped	2 tbsp. olive oil
2 carrots, pared, chopped fine	2 tbsp. lemon juice
½ red pepper, chopped	2 garlic cloves, minced
½ green pepper, chopped	salt, pepper to taste
romaine lettuce, washed, drained	a dash of hot red pepper flakes (optional)

Lay a bed of romaine lettuce on each salad plate. In a medium bowl, mix beans, onion, carrots, garlic, peppers and parsley. Blend olive oil, lemon juice, salt and pepper to taste (and red pepper flakes). Pour over bean mix; toss to mix. Spoon a serving of beans onto the bed of romaine lettuce. Serves 4-5.

....

STUFFED RED SNAPPER AND STIR-FRY NOODLES

6 medium-size fillets of red snapper, skin and bones removed
6 small skewers

FILLING:
1 ½ cups unseasoned bread crumbs
¼ cup Parmesan cheese, grated
1 tbsp. chopped Italian parsley
2 garlic cloves, peeled, minced
¼ cup raisins
¼ cup olive oil
salt and pepper to taste

TOPPING:
½ cup canned plum tomatoes, mashed
1 tbsp. chopped onion
1 tbsp. chopped Italian parsley
1 garlic clove, minced
salt and pepper to taste

In a small bowl, mix mashed plum tomatoes, onion, garlic, parsley, salt and pepper and set aside. Prepare filling: combine crumbs, cheese, parsley, garlic, raisins, salt, pepper and oil. Preheat oven to 350° F. Coat bottom of 9x13 metal pan with olive oil. Lay fillets on a sheet of waxed paper. Spoon a portion of filling on one-half of the fillet; fold over and pinch together with small metal skewer. Lay fillets in oiled pan. Spoon a portion of the tomato topping over each fillet. Bake uncovered at 350° F for 30-35 minutes. Halfway through cooking, check the bottom of the pan and add a few tablespoons of water if necessary. Serve with noodles (see next page). Serves 4-6.

....

STIR-FRY NOODLES

8 oz. fettuccine (par-cook in salted water – 2 minutes less than al dente, according to
    directions on package)
$\frac{1}{4}$ cup olive oil
2 cups broccoli florets (2-3 each serving)
$\frac{1}{4}$ cup chopped walnuts
$\frac{1}{2}$ cup unseasoned bread crumbs
$\frac{1}{2}$ tsp. salt
black pepper to taste
$\frac{1}{2}$ cup grated Parmesan cheese

Cook the pasta 1-2 minutes before al dente. Drain. Add oil to wok or skillet. Bring to
high heat. Add broccoli and walnuts and stir fry for 1-2 minutes. Pour pasta, crumbs, salt
and pepper into wok; stirring quickly, cook pasta for another 1-2 minutes. Pour mix into
a large serving bowl. Grate Parmesan over pasta mix and serve immediately. Serves 4-6.

……………………………..

COFFEE MARSHMALLOW CREAM

1 lb. marshmallows, cut into small chunks (use scissors)
1 cup strong coffee
1 pt. heavy cream, whipped to stiff peaks
$\frac{1}{4}$ cup chopped walnuts

Melt marshmallows in top part of 2-qt. double boiler, stirring constantly as they melt.
Pour coffee over marshmallows; stir to blend. Remove from heat. Cool slightly. Fold in
whipped cream. Spoon into large dessert bowls; chill for 1-2 hours. Sprinkle with
walnuts at serving time. Serves 4-5.

✿✿✿✿✿✿✿✿✿✿

Red Potato, Green Beans and Roasted Pepper
Filet Mignon Wrapped in Bacon
Apple Walnut Pudding

✩ ✩ ✩ ✩ ✩ ✩ ✩ ✩ ✩ ✩

RED POTATO, GREEN BEANS AND ROASTED PEPPER

3-4 red Bliss potatoes, scrubbed, pare some skin, cut potatoes into small chunks
3 cups green beans, trimmed, rinsed
2 large red peppers, roasted, skin peeled, seeded, sliced thin
    (see page 13 on "How to Roast Peppers")
4-6 white mushrooms, cleaned, thinly sliced
1 small onion, thinly sliced
3-4 garlic cloves, chopped
2 tbsp. olive oil
1 tbsp. dried oregano
$\frac{1}{4}$ tsp. black pepper
$\frac{1}{4}$ tsp. salt
$\frac{1}{2}$ cup pitted oil-cured black olives

Add one cup of water to 2-quart steamer pot. Place potato chunks and green beans in steamer basket. Cover and bring to a boil; lower heat and simmer for 5 minutes. Remove basket from pot and set aside with vegetables. In a large skillet, lightly brown onions and garlic in 2 tablespoons of olive oil. Add par-boiled potato-green bean mix; stir-fry for 3-4 minutes, scraping bottom of skillet. Add sliced mushroom for last minute. Transfer to a large heat-resistant serving platter. Add prepared strips of roasted peppers and olives. Sprinkle with oregano, salt and pepper. Toss well. Serve warm. Serves 4-6.

FILET MIGNON WRAPPED IN BACON

4-6 filet mignons, center cut, 1 $\frac{1}{2}$-2 inches thick
4-6 strips lean pork bacon
black pepper to taste
4-6 small metal skewers

(This beef cut needs no marinade.)
Preheat grill or broiler to 500° F. Wrap each filet around the edges with a strip of lean bacon. Insert a small metal skewer to hold bacon in place. Do not use wood toothpicks. Broil at 500° F about 3 minutes on each side (meat thermometer should register 140° F for rare; 160° F for medium-rare; dare I say it–170° F for well-done). Remove skewers and serve with salad. Pepper to taste. Serves 4-6.

…………………………..

APPLE WALNUT PUDDING

4 oz. butter or Smart Balance Spread
6 tbsp. flour
2 tsp. baking powder
1 tsp. ground cinnamon
$\frac{1}{2}$ tsp. salt
$\frac{1}{2}$ cup light brown sugar
6 eggs, or 1 $\frac{1}{2}$ cups egg substitute, beaten
1 tbsp. vanilla extract
1 tbsp. lemon juice
1 cup chopped walnuts
3-4 large cooking apples: Rome Beauty or Granny Smith, peeled, cored, chopped
vanilla ice cream

Preheat oven to 350° F. Grease a 10-inch round tin. In a large bowl, cream butter with sugar; beat in eggs. Stir in flour with baking powder, cinnamon and salt. Stir in vanilla; fold in chopped apples and walnuts. Pour into greased pan and bake at 350° F for 35-40 minutes until lightly golden and toothpick removes clean. Serve warm with a dollop of vanilla ice cream. Serves 4-5.

✿✿✿✿✿✿✿✿✿✿

SUMMER–FALL

Herbed Corn and Tomato Chowder
Cucumber and Tomato Salad
Seafood Stuffed Mushrooms
The Banana Bowl

✿✿✿✿✿✿✿✿✿✿

HERBED CORN AND TOMATO CHOWDER

2 slices cooked bacon, crumbled
1 can (1 lb.) corn kernels. drained
2 tsp. olive oil
1 large onion, chopped
2 carrots, pared, sliced in $\frac{1}{4}$-inch rounds
1 large stalk celery, cleaned, cut into $\frac{1}{4}$-inch chunks
2-3 small boiled potatoes, peeled, cut into 1-inch cubes
2 cups chicken consommé, canned; or mash 2 chicken bouillon cubes
    in 2 cups boiling water
1 tsp. oregano
1 tsp. thyme
$\frac{1}{2}$ tsp. salt
$\frac{1}{4}$ tsp. black pepper
dash of Tabasco sauce (to taste)
$\frac{1}{2}$ cup canned stewing tomatoes
2 cups low fat milk or fat-free evaporated milk

In a large soup pot, brown onions in 2 teaspoons olive oil. Scrape bottom of pot. Pour in consommé. Stir in carrots, celery, tomato and potatoes. Cover and bring to boil; simmer for 7-10 minutes. Stir in crumbled bacon, oregano, thyme, corn, salt, pepper, Tabasco and milk. Cover and simmer for another 5 minutes, stirring occasionally, until soup thickens. Serve with baking powder biscuits. Serves 4-5.

………………………………..

CUCUMBER AND TOMATO SALAD

1 seedless Asian cucumber, skin scraped, sliced in thin rounds
2 chilled tomatoes, thinly sliced in rounds
3-4 leaves torn basil
1 tsp. dried oregano
Spicy Salad Dressing (see page 175)

On a flat serving platter, arrange a layer of thinly sliced tomatoes, followed by a layer of cucumber rounds. Sprinkle oregano and torn basil over salad. Drizzle with Spicy Salad Dressing. Serve immediately. Serves 4-5.

....

SEAFOOD STUFFED MUSHROOMS

1 doz. large mushrooms for stuffing
1 lb. large shrimp, peeled, cleaned, rinsed, drained
1 lb. bay scallops, rinsed, drained
1 cup unseasoned bread crumbs
1 tbsp. fresh parsley, chopped
2 garlic cloves, minced
1 stalk celery, minced
4 tbsp. olive oil
2 tbsp. water
few dashes Tabasco sauce
$\frac{1}{2}$ tsp. salt
$\frac{1}{4}$ tsp. black pepper
$\frac{1}{4}$ cup mushroom stems, chopped
Hungarian paprika
olive oil for sprinkling
oil to coat pan

Preheat oven to 375° F. In a medium bowl, combine crumbs, scallops, parsley, garlic, celery, mushroom stems, salt, pepper, Tabasco, olive oil and water. In a 9x13-inch oil-coated baking pan, arrange mushrooms. First, stuff 1 tablespoon crumb-scallop mix into each mushroom cavity. Then press 1-2 shrimps into the crumbs of each mushroom, head first, with shrimp tail protruding from each mushroom. Sprinkle olive oil and paprika over mushrooms and bake at 375° F for 20-25 minutes. Serves 4-5.

....

THE BANANA BOWL

4-6 waffle bowls – purchased in supermarkets in ice cream section
1 qt. vanilla ice cream
2 large bananas, sliced in $\frac{1}{4}$ -inch rounds
1 cup sliced strawberries
1 pt. heavy cream for whipping
chocolate fudge sauce
4-5 tbsp. pecans

Place waffle bowls in individual dessert bowls. Beat cream into stiff peaks. Add a layer of sliced bananas at bottom of waffle bowls. Scoop a portion of ice cream on bananas. Scatter sliced strawberries over ice cream. Then, top with fudge sauce, a dollop of whipped cream and pecans.

✿✿✿✿✿✿✿✿✿

Ceci and Gorgonzola Salad
Pork Tenderloin Baguettes
Roasted Baby Artichokes
A Loaf of Chocolate

✧ ✧ ✧ ✧ ✧ ✧ ✧ ✧ ✧ ✧

CECI AND GORGONZOLA SALAD

1 large can (1 ½ lbs.) ceci, rinsed,
   drained
4 garlic cloves, peeled, chopped
4 scallions cleaned, cut into ½-inch
   pieces, including greens
1 cup crumbled Gorgonzola cheese
2-3 fresh plum tomatoes, cut in rounds

1 tbsp. Italian parsley, chopped
½ cup Sicilian olives, pitted, sliced
Honey Mustard Dressing for basting
   (see page 173)
large leaves of Boston lettuce, washed,
   drained

Set a leaf of lettuce into each salad bowl. In a medium-size bowl mix ceci, garlic, gorgonzola, scallions, tomatoes, parsley and olives. Refrigerate. At serving time, add Honey Mustard Dressing; stir to mix. Spoon into salad bowls. Serves 4.

………………………………..

PORK TENDERLOIN BAGUETTES

4-5 pork tenderloin, ½-inch thick, trimmed
Honey Mustard Dressing for basting (see page 173)
1 cup corn flake crumbs
½ tsp. black pepper
1 tsp. each: onion powder, powered cumin
olive oil to coat pan
½ cup Calamata olives, pitted
2 red peppers, seeded, roasted (see page 13 for directions on "How to Roast Peppers")
4-5 soft sandwich baguettes, sliced in half

Preheat oven to 400° F. Spray to coat a 7x9 non-stick pan. Roast peppers and set aside. On a sheet of waxed paper, pour corn flake crumbs mixed with cumin, pepper and onion powder. Brush pork with Honey Mustard Dressing; coat each tenderloin in crumbs; lay them side by side in prepared pan. Roast uncovered at 400° F for 15-20 minutes, dependent on thickness, turning once during that time. Cut baguettes in half, lengthwise and stuff with a piece of pork and a strip or two of roasted pepper and a spoonful of olives. Serve immediately with salad. Serves 4-5.

………………………………..

ROASTED BABY ARTICHOKES

(May be prepared in advance and refrigerated. Cover with foil and warm thoroughly before serving.)

6-8 small globe artichokes, cut off base; cut off about $\frac{1}{2}$-inch top (leaves), trim, wash, drain
$\frac{1}{4}$ cup lemon juice
1 cup cold water

STUFFING:
1 cup unseasoned bread crumbs
6-8 garlic cloves, peeled, halved (set aside 6-8 halves and chop remainder of cloves)
1 tbsp. fresh parsley, chopped
$\frac{1}{4}$ tsp. black pepper, $\frac{1}{2}$ tsp. salt
$\frac{1}{4}$ cup grated Provolone cheese
$\frac{1}{4}$ cup olive oil
(more oil for sprinkling and for the pot – about 2 tablespoons)

Preheat oven to 350° F. Prepare artichokes as directed (above). Carefully, spread each artichoke and snip off pinchy tops of inner leaves with scissors. Place artichokes in a medium-size pan (5x7). Mix lemon juice into 1 cup cold water and pour into the bottom of the pan, about one-half inch high. Add a little more water if necessary. Prepare the stuffing: in a bowl, combine crumbs, chopped garlic, parsley, cheese, pepper and salt. Add oil; mix to moisten. Divide stuffing among the artichokes, packing about 1 tablespoon stuffing into each cavity. Return each stuffed artichoke to pan with lemon juice and water. Drizzle 2 tablespoonfuls olive oil into and among artichokes; make certain some oil is added to water mix. Loosely cover pot of artichokes with a sheet of foil. Roast in preheated oven at 350° F for 40 minutes. Baste with water mix from pot. Reform foil into a tent and continue to roast artichokes for another 10 minutes.
Tops should be golden brown. Test for doneness by pulling out an end- leaf to taste. Texture should be lightly firm, not mushy.

....

A LOAF OF CHOCOLATE
(Prepare a day or two in advance.)

6 oz. dark chocolate, cut into small pieces (or chocolate morsels)
6 tbsp. canola oil or unsalted butter
1 can (7 $\frac{1}{2}$ oz.) condensed milk
2 tsp. ground cinnamon
$\frac{1}{4}$ cup chopped almonds with skin
1 cup almond cookies, crumbled
$\frac{1}{4}$ cup dried apricots, chopped

Line a 5x7 loaf pan with foil. In top pot of medium-size double-boiler, combine oil
(or butter), chocolate pieces, milk and cinnamon and gently melt the chocolate mix over
hot water, stirring often with a wooden spoon until the chocolate has melted.
Remove pot from stove and beat the mixture well. Stir in almonds, cookies and apricots.
Pour the chocolate mix into the prepared pan. Refrigerate for at least 1-2 hours or until
set. Before serving, remove loaf from pan to cutting board and peel off foil. Cut the
chocolate loaf into slices and serve with a cup of richly brewed coffee. Serves 12 slices.

✿✿✿✿✿✿✿✿✿✿

SUMMER–FALL

Salad of Arugula, Radicchio and Endive
Cinnamon Chicken
Noodle Pudding

✿ ✿ ✿ ✿ ✿ ✿ ✿ ✿ ✿

SALAD OF ARUGULA, RADICCHIO AND ENDIVE

1 bunch arugula, cut into bite-size pieces, rinsed, dried
1 small head radicchio, trimmed, torn into bite-size
4-6 small white mushrooms, rinsed, sliced thin
2 endives, trimmed, cut crosswise into 1-inch pieces and leaves separated
1 carrot, peeled, shredded
Spicy Salad Dressing (see page 175)

In a large salad bowl, toss all vegetables to mix. Refrigerate. At serving time, drizzle
Spicy Salad Dressing over salad, and toss well. Serves 4-6.

....

CINNAMON CHICKEN
(Start day before.)

4-6 pieces boned, skinned chicken
   breast, washed, patted dry with
   paper towel
$\frac{1}{3}$ cup sherry
$\frac{1}{3}$ cup honey
2 tsp. ground cinnamon
2 tbsp. lemon juice
1 tsp. curry powder

2-3 garlic cloves, minced
$\frac{1}{2}$ tsp. salt
$\frac{1}{4}$ tsp. black pepper
2 tbsp. olive oil
2 cups broccoli florets
8 small white mushrooms, rinsed,
   quartered
$\frac{1}{2}$ cup walnut halves

Preheat oven to 375° F. Blend all the marinade ingredients in a bowl and mix thoroughly.
Baste chicken on both sides with sherry-cinnamon mix. Pour rest of marinade over
chicken in a 9x13 Pyrex casserole. Cover with plastic and let stand in refrigerator for
several hours or over night. Bake uncovered at 375° F for about 55 minutes –1 hour.
After 35 minutes, add walnuts, broccoli florets and mushrooms to the Pyrex and baste
with marinade. Continue to baste occasionally. Serves 4-6.

....

NOODLE PUDDING (NEAPOLITAN PASTIERA)

1 lb. par-boiled spaghetti, drained
¼ cup finely chopped citron
¼ cup white raisins
6 large eggs, beaten (or 1 ½ cups egg substitute)
1 lb. ricotta (you may use whole or skim milk)
1 tsp. ground cinnamon
½ cup granulated sugar
black pepper, salt to taste
1 tbsp. butter, small cubes (or Smart Balance)
more butter to coat 9x13 Pyrex dish

Preheat oven to 375° F. Butter a 9x13-inch Pyrex casserole dish. Pour the par-boiled spaghetti into a large bowl; stir in beaten eggs, ricotta, citron, raisins, sugar, cinnamon, pepper and salt. Pour this mix into the buttered casserole dish. Dot with butter. Bake at 375° F for 25 minutes, or until lightly browned. Cut into wedges. Delicious warm or at room temperature. Try this recipe with whole wheat pasta for a nutty taste. Serves 6.

✿✿✿✿✿✿✿✿✿

SUMMER–FALL

Spinach and Feta Salad with Figs
Shrimp Scorpio
Coffee Sundae

❋❋❋❋❋❋❋❋❋

SPINACH AND FETA SALAD WITH FIGS

4 cups baby spinach, rinsed, dried
1 large carrot, pared and shredded
4 garlic cloves, chopped
4-6 fresh figs (Brown Turkey, Kadota or Calimyrna), washed, trimmed, quartered
½ pt. blueberries, rinsed, drained
1 cup feta cheese, crumbled
Vinaigrette Dressing (see page 177)

Prepare Vinaigrette Dressing. In a large salad bowl, mix spinach, carrot, garlic, figs, blueberries and feta. Refrigerate until serving. Toss with dressing. Serves 4-5.

…………………………..

SHRIMP SCORPIO
(May be prepared ahead of time.)

2 lbs. large shrimp, cleaned, peeled,
    rinsed and drained
¼ cup olive oil
2 onions, chopped fine
3-4 garlic cloves, chopped
¼ cup fresh parsley, chopped

1 tbsp. dried dill weed
¼ tsp. dry mustard
½ tsp. granulated sugar
2 cups canned plum tomatoes, mashed
1 cup feta cheese, crumbled
salt, pepper to taste

Preheat oven to 425° F. In a large saucepan, heat oil and brown onions and garlic. Add parsley and dill, mustard and sugar, salt and pepper and mashed plum tomatoes. Simmer for 20 minutes. Add shrimp to sauce; cook about 5 minutes or until shrimp are almost done; do not over cook. Pour mixture into an oven-proof casserole; sprinkle with crumbled feta. Bake, uncovered, for 10-15 minutes at 425° F, or until cheese is melted. Serve over rice (see next page). Serves 4-5.

…………………………..

STEAMED RICE:

Add 1 cup arborio rice to 2 $\frac{1}{2}$ cups boiling water; add 1 tablespoon olive oil, salt and pepper to taste and simmer, covered, for 20-25 minutes, until water is almost absorbed. Spoon into serving dishes and ladle Shrimp Scorpio over rice.

………………………………..

COFFEE SUNDAE

1 qt. coffee ice cream
$\frac{1}{4}$ cup chocolate truffle sauce or fudge sauce
4 tbsp. ouzo or anisette
heavy cream for whipping
$\frac{1}{4}$ cup tiny semi-sweet chocolate morsels

Blend ouzo and chocolate sauce in a small bowl. Whip cream to form peaks. Refrigerate. At serving time, scoop one portion of coffee ice cream into sundae glasses. Drizzle with ouzo sauce. Top with whipped cream and sprinkle with tiny morsels. Serve with crisp lady fingers (or Savoyard biscuits). Serves 4-5.

✿✿✿✿✿✿✿✿✿✿

SUMMER–FALL

Potato and Bacon Soup
Turkey Scallopine
Warm Beans and Pepper Salad
Chocolate Pumpkin Muffins

✧✧✧✧✧✧✧✧✧

POTATO AND BACON SOUP

6 medium all-purpose potatoes, pared, cubed, place in bowl with cold water to cover
1 large onion, chopped
4 slices lean bacon, cooked, drained on paper towel, set aside
2 tbsp. olive oil
1 pt. sour cream
1 small green bell pepper, cored, seeded, chopped
4 cups chicken stock (use canned consommé or mash and dissolve 4 chicken bouillon
     cubes in 4 cups of boiling water)
1 tsp. nutmeg
1 tsp. salt
½ tsp. black pepper
cayenne pepper for sprinkling

Drain potatoes. Brown cubed potatoes and onion in 2 tablespoons of hot olive oil in
2 ½-quart soup pot. Add prepared stock; stir, scraping bottom of pot. Add green pepper,
salt, pepper and nutmeg and bring pot to simmer, covered, for 20 minutes. Stir in sour
cream; crumble bacon and add to soup. Simmer soup for another 5-10 minutes.
Pour into soup tureen; sprinkle with cayenne to taste. Serves 4-5.

....

TURKEY SCALLOPINE

4-6 turkey cutlets
1 cup flour
1 tbsp. dried oregano
1 tsp. salt
$\frac{1}{4}$ tsp. black pepper
4 tbsp. olive oil

$\frac{1}{4}$ cup dry white wine
$\frac{1}{4}$ cup lemon juice
2 tbsp. Italian parsley, chopped
2 tbsp. capers, drained
8-10 thin slices of lemon

Mix flour with salt, pepper, oregano on a large sheet of waxed paper. Heat oil in large skillet (about 320° F). Dredge cutlets in flour mix to coat both sides. Cook cutlets in skillet, 2 at a time, on each side, until golden and cooked through (a couple of minutes on each side). Transfer to warm serving platter. Leave a couple of tablespoonfuls hot oil in skillet; stir in wine and juice and simmer for 1 minute. Stir in capers and parsley and lemon slices and cook for another minute. Spoon lemon slices and sauce onto cutlets. Serves 4-5.

....

WARM BEANS AND PEPPER SALAD

2-3 large roasted red peppers (see page 13 "How to Roast Peppers")
2 $\frac{1}{2}$ cups green beans, trimmed, cut into 2 inch pieces, steamed for 4-5 minutes
2 tbsp. olive oil
2 garlic cloves, minced
$\frac{1}{2}$ tsp. salt
$\frac{1}{4}$ tsp. black pepper
1 tbsp. dried oregano
$\frac{1}{4}$ cup pitted and chopped calamata olives

Slice roasted peppers. Pour cooked beans into medium-size serving bowl. Drizzle olive oil over beans; add salt and pepper, garlic and oregano and toss to mix. Lay strips of red peppers over bean salad. Sprinkle with chopped olives. Serve warm. Serves 4-5.

....

CHOCOLATE PUMPKIN MUFFINS
(Prepare day or two before.)

1 box chocolate cake mix (about 22 oz.)
1 cup canned pumpkin
1 cup fat-free evaporated milk
1 tbsp. ground cinnamon
$\frac{1}{2}$ pt fresh raspberries, gently rinsed, drained
1 cup semi-sweet chocolate morsels
confectioners' sugar for dusting

Grease 6-7 Texas-size muffin cups. Preheat oven to 350° F. In a large bowl, combine cake mix, pumpkin, milk and cinnamon. Beat until smooth. Stir in raspberries. Spoon batter into prepared muffin cups. Dot tops with chocolate morsels. Bake in preheated oven 350° F for about 30 minutes or until inserted toothpick comes out clean. Cool muffins thoroughly. Remove from muffin cups. Refrigerate until 2 hours before serving. Dust with confectioners' sugar just before serving.

✿✿✿✿✿✿✿✿✿

Chicory, Red-Leaf and Carrot Salad
Pasta with Chicken Sausage in Three-Cheese Sauce
Chocolate Amaretto Cupcakes

✿ ✿ ✿ ✿ ✿ ✿ ✿ ✿ ✿

CHICORY, RED-LEAF AND CARROT SALAD

2 cups chicory (or frisée), trimmed, drained, cut into pieces
2 cups torn red leaf lettuce, rinsed, drained
1-2 carrots, pared, shredded
1 small red onion, thinly sliced
Italian Dressing (see page 173)

In a large salad bowl combine chicory, red leaf, carrots and onion. Refrigerate.
Before serving, drizzle Italian Dressing over salad, toss and serve. Serves 4-5.

....

PASTA WITH CHICKEN SAUSAGE IN THREE-CHEESE SAUCE

8 oz. pasta: rotini, bowties or cut ziti,
    cook according to directions on
    package; drain, and return to
    pasta pot
2 cups broccoli florets
6-8 small mushrooms, quartered
½ cup chopped red pepper
½ cup chopped green pepper
4-6 links chicken sausage

SAUCE:
4 tbsp. olive oil
4 tbsp. flour
1 ½ cups (1 can) evaporated milk,
    (fat-free)
½ tsp. salt
¼ tsp. black pepper
1 tbsp. Worcestershire sauce
2-3 dashes Tabasco sauce
1 tbsp. mustard spread
¼ cup each: Parmesan, Asiago,
    Romano cheeses, grated

Preheat oven to 375° F. Brown sausage in skillet in 4 tablespoons olive oil. Remove sausage to plate. At low heat in same skillet, stir 4 tablespoons of flour into scrapings. Add milk, salt and pepper, sauces and mustard spread. Stir until smooth. Add grated cheeses and continue to cook, stirring until blended. Turn off heat. Have a greased oven-resistant 9x13-inch casserole pan ready. Pour one-half cheese sauce into drained pasta in pot and toss to mix. Add broccoli, mushrooms, chopped peppers to pasta. Pour the remaining cheese sauce into pasta pot and blend thoroughly. Pour and spread the pasta mix into the greased casserole pan. Arrange the cooked sausage into the pasta mix. Bake, covered with a sheet of foil at 375° F for 30 minutes. Remove foil and continue to bake for 10 minutes longer. Serves 4-6.

……………………………..

CHOCOLATE AMARETTO CUPCAKES
(Prepare day before.)

1 pkg. (18 oz.) chocolate cake mix
1 pkg. (3 $\frac{1}{2}$ oz.) chocolate instant pudding mix
4 eggs beaten, or 1 cup egg substitute
$\frac{1}{2}$ cup amaretto liqueur, 1 tsp. nutmeg
$\frac{1}{2}$ cup water
$\frac{1}{2}$ cup apple sauce
$\frac{1}{2}$ cup sliced almonds
confectioners' sugar for dusting

Preheat oven to 350° F. Grease non-stick muffin pan, (Texas-size muffins). Sprinkle bottoms of cups with sliced almonds. In a large mixing bowl, prepare batter. Combine cake mix and instant pudding. Add beaten eggs and beat at medium speed to blend. Add liquids and apple sauce and nutmeg. Beat at medium-high speed for 5 minutes. Pour about one-half cupful of batter into each large muffin cup (about one-half full). Bake in preheated oven 350° F for 25 minutes or until toothpick tests clean. Do not under bake. Remove from oven and let cool for 10 minutes. Turn out muffins to a doily-lined serving dish. Before serving, sprinkle cupcakes with confectioners' sugar. Yields 5-6 large muffins.

✧✧✧✧✧✧✧✧✧✧

Red Cabbage and Apple Slaw
Seafood Polenta
Orange Tapioca

✿✿✿✿✿✿✿✿✿✿

RED CABBAGE AND APPLE SLAW

4 cups red cabbage, shredded
2 small or 1 large Granny Smith apple, cored, chopped fine (do not remove skin)
2 stalks celery, chopped fine
$\frac{1}{4}$ cup mayonnaise
$\frac{1}{4}$ cup plain yogurt
2 tbsp. white vinegar
juice of 1 lemon
$\frac{1}{2}$ tsp. granulated sugar
1 tbsp. prepared hot horseradish

Combine cabbage, apple and celery in a large salad bowl. In a small bowl, thoroughly
blend mayonnaise, yogurt, vinegar, lemon juice, sugar and prepared horseradish.
Pour over salad and toss to combine. Serves 4-5.

………………………………..

SEAFOOD POLENTA

1 lb. large shrimp, peeled, cleaned, rinsed, drained
1 lb. bay scallops (or use quartered sea scallops)
1 lb. fresh tuna, remove skin, cut into 1-inch chunks (you can substitute a thick firm
    fleshy fish such as swordfish or halibut)
4-6 strips bacon
1 lb. slice of cured ham ($\frac{1}{2}$-inch thick), diced
1 onion, minced
4-6 small white mushrooms, rinsed, chopped
$\frac{1}{4}$ cup tomato purée
$\frac{1}{2}$ cup water
$\frac{1}{4}$ cup chopped fresh basil
$\frac{1}{2}$ tsp. black pepper
$\frac{1}{2}$ tsp. salt
$\frac{1}{2}$ cup yellow cornmeal, fine
2 cups boiling water

Preheat oven 350° F. In 2–quart pot, pour boiling water over cornmeal and simmer gently, while stirring, until thick. Set aside. Fry bacon in skillet until crisp; remove from skillet and set on paper towels to absorb fat. Remove all but one tablespoon of bacon fat from skillet. Add onion and cook on high heat for 2 minutes, scraping bottom of skillet. Lower heat and add tomato, $\frac{1}{2}$ cup water, mushrooms, ham, basil, salt and pepper. Stir to blend and simmer for 10 minutes. Turn off heat under skillet; crumble bacon and stir into cooked cornmeal. Grease a 9x12-inch oven-proof casserole dish. Add shrimp, scallops and tuna chunks to bowl with tomato sauce. Stir to blend. Spoon one-third of the tomato-seafood mix on bottom of casserole. Next, spoon one-half the polenta mix over tomato-seafood mix. Spoon another third of tomato-seafood mix; then make a layer with the polenta. Lastly, spoon the remainder of the sauce over the seafood polenta and cover dish with a piece of foil. Bake at 350° F for 30 minutes. Cut into 4x6 sections. Use spatula to remove portions. Serve hot. Makes 4 portions.

....

ORANGE TAPIOCA
(Start day before.)

$\frac{1}{2}$ cup small pearl Tapioca, 2 cups water
2 $\frac{1}{2}$ cups low fat milk
$\frac{1}{4}$ tsp. salt
2 eggs, separated
$\frac{1}{2}$ tsp. vanilla extract
$\frac{1}{2}$ cup granulated sugar
1 small can mandarin oranges, drained
$\frac{1}{2}$ pt. blueberries, rinsed and drained
$\frac{1}{4}$ cup white raisins soaked in 2 tbsp. Grand Marnier
ground nutmeg for sprinkling

Soak tapioca in 2 cups water, overnight. Drain water. Soak raisins in Grand Marnier. Set aside. Pour 1 cup water in bottom of 2-quart double boiler. Turn up heat to medium. In top pot, heat milk until just warm. Add tapioca and salt. Continue heating until small bubbles form at sides of pot. Stir the tapioca. Cover with lid; turn heat to very low and cook for 1 hour, stirring frequently. Be sure mixture does not boil or simmer. Meanwhile, separate egg whites from yolks. Beat yolks and sugar together until light yellow in color. Add a little of the hot tapioca mixture to the yolks and blend thoroughly. Then, blend this yolk mix into the rest of the hot tapioca mix, stirring constantly. Turn heat to medium under the double boiler and continue to cook until tapioca is very thick, about 15 minutes. Beat egg whites until stiff. Stir raisins, blueberries and oranges into tapioca mix. Slowly fold the egg whites into the tapioca. Stir in vanilla. Pour into 2-quart glass bowl; sprinkle with nutmeg. Serve warm or chilled. Serves 4-5.

✧✧✧✧✧✧✧✧✧✧

Waldorf Salad with Grapes and Apples
Sausage Jambalaya
Sweet and Tart Stewed Fruit

✧✧✧✧✧✧✧✧✧✧

WALDORF SALAD WITH GRAPES AND APPLES

3 cups torn greenleaf lettuce, washed, drained
1 cup celery, diced
1 cup diced apples, cored, do not pare
1 cup red seedless grapes
½ cup chopped walnuts
1 cup mayonnaise
¼ tsp. black pepper
juice of 1 lemon

In a small bowl, blend mayonnaise, lemon juice and black pepper. In a large salad bowl, combine lettuce, celery, apples, grapes and walnuts. Pour dressing over salad. Toss to mix thoroughly. Serves 4-5.

…………………………………..

SAUSAGE JAMBALAYA

4 tbsp. olive oil
1 large onion, chopped
2-3 garlic cloves, chopped
1 green pepper, seeded and chopped
1 red pepper, seeded and chopped
1 small chile or pimiento pepper, seeded
   and chopped (use plastic gloves
   when handling hot pepper)

2 cups canned plum tomatoes, mashed
¼ cup dry white wine
1 tsp. salt
¼ tsp. black pepper
¼ cup chopped fresh parsley
1 tbsp. dried thyme
6 links chorizo sausage
white rice for accompaniment

Brown onion, garlic and sausage in oil in a large skillet at medium-high 320° F. Lower heat and scrape bottom of pan. Add green and red peppers and chile and sauté for 1-2 minutes. Add tomatoes, wine, salt, pepper and herbs. Cover skillet and simmer for 20-25 minutes. Meanwhile, combine ½ cup long grain rice in 2 cups of boiling water in a 1-quart saucepot. Cover pot and simmer for 20 minutes or until water is just absorbed. Pour jambalaya into a large, round casserole for serving. Spoon the cooked rice around the edge of the casserole with the sausages and sauce in the center. Serves 4-6.

…………………………………..

SWEET AND TART STEWED FRUIT

2 grapefruit, remove rind; section the grapefruit and place in large serving bowl

3 oranges, remove rind; section the oranges and place in same serving bowl

1 large can (29 oz.) Elberta peach halves, drain and add to serving bowl (save the juice)

1 large can (15 oz.) pineapple chunks; or use fresh pineapple, rind removed and cut into small chunks (save the juice) – add chunks to bowl

1 cup white raisins

1 cup pitted whole prunes

1 cup brown sugar

juice from cans of peaches and pineapple

¼ cup rum

Use heat-resistant serving bowl for fruit. In a 1-quart saucepan, stir and blend sugar into water; add fruit juice and rum. Bring to a boil; then, simmer for 5 minutes; stir in raisins and prunes and simmer for another 5 minutes. Pour over the fruit in the serving bowl. Stir to blend. Serve warm or chilled. Serves 4-5.

✿✿✿✿✿✿✿✿✿

Mixed Green with Bleu Cheese Vinaigrette
Burger Soup
Angelic Cake

✧✧✧✧✧✧✧✧✧✧

MIXED GREENS WITH BLEU CHEESE VINAIGRETTE

1 cup torn red leaf lettuce
1 cup torn romaine
1 cup cut escarole; use center of bunch
1 cup baby spinach
1 small head cut radicchio
1 small red onion, thinly sliced
add ¼ cup crumbled bleu cheese to dressing
Vinaigrette Dressing (see page 177)

Wash and thoroughly drain all salad ingredients. Combine in large salad bowl. Add bleu cheese to dressing. Pour on salad and toss, just before serving. Serves 4-5.

……………………………..

BURGER SOUP

1 lb. lean ground beef
1 lb. Italian sweet sausage meat
1 onion, chopped
1-2 carrots, pared, sliced in thin rounds
½ cup green beans, cut into pieces, rinsed
1 large stalk celery, chopped fine
1-2 all-purpose potatoes, pared, cut into small chunks
2 garlic cloves, chopped
1 small can (10 oz.) corn kernels, rinsed, drained

1 can (1 lb.) plum tomatoes in sauce, mashed
6 cups water
1 tbsp. Worcestershire sauce
1 tsp. salt
½ tsp. black pepper
1 bay leaf
1 tbsp. dried oregano
1 tbsp. chopped basil
¼ cup rice
2 tbsp. olive oil

In a large soup pot with lid, preferably non-stick, heat oil and cook onion, garlic, ground beef and sausage meat until beef and sausage meat are just cooked. Scrape all food particles from bottom of pot. Add carrots, celery, beans and potatoes. Stir in tomatoes, water and Worcestershire sauce, salt, pepper and herbs. Cover and cook to simmer for 15 minutes. Stir in rice, while soup simmers; cover and continue to simmer for another 20-25 minutes, stirring occasionally. Stir corn kernels into soup and continue to simmer another 10 minutes. Add more salt and pepper as desired. Serve with frizelle biscuits. Serves 6.

....

ANGELIC CAKE

6 egg whites
2 ½ cups granulated sugar
4 cups ground almonds (use food processor)
1 ½ cups flour
1 cup butter or Smart Balance spread

Preheat oven 350° F. In a large bowl, beat egg whites with electric beater until firm. Slowly add sugar while beating. Stiff peaks should form. Fold in flour and ground almonds. Melt butter; cool. Fold butter into mixture. Pour the batter into a 10-inch round, ungreased cake pan, preferably non-stick. Bake at 350° F on lowest rack for 1 ½ hours, or until inserted toothpick comes out clean. Serve with a demitasse of Italian coffee.

✿✿✿✿✿✿✿✿✿✿

Escarole, Frisée and Cashews
Spicy Chicken and Vegetables
Pumpkin Cake

✿✿✿✿✿✿✿✿✿✿

ESCAROLE, FRISÉE AND CASHEWS

2 cups cut escarole (use center of bunch), rinsed, drained
2 cups torn frisée (or chicory), rinsed and drained
1 large carrot, pared, shredded
½ cup dried cranberries
¼ cup cashews, chopped fine
Honey Mustard Dressing (see page 173)

Combine escarole, frisée, carrots, dried cranberries and nuts in a large salad bowl. Refrigerate. Prepare Honey Mustard Dressing. Drizzle over salad just before serving and toss to mix. Serves 4-5.

....

SPICY CHICKEN AND VEGETABLES

4-6 chicken breast halves, boned,
   skinned
4 garlic cloves, minced
$\frac{1}{2}$ tsp. ground ginger
$\frac{1}{2}$ tsp. cinnamon
4 tbsp. olive oil
juice of 2 oranges
juice of 1 lemon
1 tbsp. grated orange peel
1 tsp. grated lemon peel

1 tbsp. grated ginger root
1 tbsp. honey
1 cup chicken stock (canned consommé)
1 tsp. salt
$\frac{1}{2}$ tsp. black pepper
1 tsp. coriander leaves
1 tsp. chopped parsley
2 cupfuls broccoli florets, rinsed, drained
8 small white mushrooms, rinsed,
   drained

Wash chicken, pat dry with paper towels. Blend garlic, ginger and cinnamon and rub it over chicken. Heat oil in a heavy skillet (with a cover). Add the chicken and brown on both sides. Mix the juices with the grated rinds, ginger, honey and stock. Pour this mix over the chicken in the skillet and bring it to a boil. Add salt and pepper and herbs. Cover the pan; lower heat and simmer gently for 20 minutes. Turn over the chicken breasts several times during cooking. Remove chicken to heat-resistant serving platter and keep warm and covered. Turn heat up under skillet and cook broccoli and mushrooms in sauce in skillet for 2-3 minutes. Spoon vegetables and sauce over chicken breasts on the platter. Serve immediately or keep covered and warm until needed. Serves 4-6.

………………………….

PUMPKIN CAKE
(Prepare day before.)

5 eggs, beaten or 1 $\frac{1}{4}$ cups egg substitute
1 cup granulated sugar
1 can (12 oz.) evaporated milk
1 can (29 oz.) pure pumpkin
1 tsp. vanilla extract
1 tsp. ground cinnamon
$\frac{1}{2}$ tsp. salt

$\frac{1}{2}$ tsp. ground ginger
$\frac{1}{2}$ tsp. ground nutmeg
1 box (20 oz.) yellow cake mix
$\frac{1}{2}$ stick unsalted butter
$\frac{1}{2}$ cup chopped pecans
$\frac{1}{2}$ pt. heavy cream for whipping
   (optional)

Preheat oven 300° F. Grease 9x13-inch Pyrex pan. Beat eggs and sugar, milk, pumpkin, vanilla, salt, cinnamon, ginger and nutmeg into a smooth batter. Pour into greased 9x13-inch Pyrex pan. Sprinkle cake mix all over top of pumpkin mix. Pinch slivers of butter from the $\frac{1}{2}$ stick and place evenly over top of cake mix. Sprinkle with chopped pecans. Bake at 300° F for 1-1 $\frac{1}{2}$ hours, or until inserted toothpick removes clean. Serve with a dollop of whipped cream.

✿✿✿✿✿✿✿✿✿✿

Seafood Stew
Fried Fish with Vegetables and Herbs
Bread and Butter Pudding

✿✿✿✿✿✿✿✿✿✿

SEAFOOD STEW

1 ½ lbs. sea scallops, rinsed, drained. halved
½ lb. medium shrimp, peeled, cleaned, rinsed, drained
1 lb. mussels, scrubbed, leave in shell
4 crab legs, rinsed
6 cups water
1 large or 2 medium all-purpose potatoes, pared, cubed
2 tbsp. olive oil
1 large onion, chopped
1 lb. pkg. frozen mixed vegetables (or: 1 lb. can less salt variety)
¼ cup tomato paste
1 tbsp. Hungarian paprika
½ tsp. caraway seeds
1 pt. sour cream
1 tsp. salt
½ tsp. black pepper

Brown onion in olive oil in a large soup pot with cover. Scrape bottom of pot.
Add 5 cups hot water. Blend tomato paste into the sixth cup of hot water and add to soup
pot. Stir in cubed potatoes and mixed vegetables; cover and bring to a boil. Lower heat
under pot and simmer for 20 minutes. Stir in paprika and caraway seed, salt and pepper.
Add all of the seafood and bring to a simmer for 5-7 minutes. Remove 2 cups of broth
from pot and transfer this hot liquid to a small bowl; stir in sour cream until smooth.
Return this mix to the soup pot and stir to blend thoroughly. Heat on low for a few
more minutes. Serves 6.

....

FRIED FISH WITH VEGETABLES AND HERBS

4-6 medium-size thick fish fillets (lemon sole or red snapper, skin removed)
juice of 2 lemons
$\frac{1}{4}$ cup mixed: dried thyme, oregano, basil, tarragon
1 tsp. salt
$\frac{1}{4}$ tsp. black pepper
$\frac{1}{4}$ cup olive oil
1 doz. asparagus spears, trimmed, rinsed
1 red pepper, cored, sliced thin
6-8 white mushrooms, sliced thin, rinsed

Lay a sheet of waxed paper on cutting board. Make a rub with salt, pepper, and all of the herbs. Coat the waxed paper with this mix. Sprinkle lemon juice on both sides of fish fillets and coat with herb rub. Heat olive oil in a large heavy skillet to 320° F. Fry the fillets 2-3 minutes on each side, depending on thickness, until just lightly crisped. Remove to heat-resistant serving platter and keep warm. Add the vegetables to the skillet. Lower heat and gently sauté mushrooms, asparagus and pepper slices for 2-3 minutes. Remove vegetables to fish platter. Serve immediately; use spatula and large spoon. Divide among 4-6 portions.

....

BREAD AND BUTTER PUDDING
(Start preparation early on the day.)

4 large slices white bread, remove crusts
2 oz. butter or Smart Balance spread
$\frac{1}{2}$ cup white raisins
4 tbsp. brown sugar
4 eggs, beaten or 1 cup egg substitute

1 $\frac{1}{4}$ pts. milk (or evaporated milk)
1 tbsp. grated lemon rind
1 tsp. ground nutmeg
1 tbsp. brown sugar
butter to grease bowl

Preheat oven to 275° F. Grease a 2-quart Pyrex bowl with some butter. Butter both sides of 4 slices uncrusted white bread with 2 ounces butter. Line the bottom of greased bowl with 2 slices of buttered bread. Sprinkle one-quarter cup raisins and 2 tablespoons of sugar over bread. Repeat with a layer of the remaining 2 slices of buttered bread; follow with remainder of raisins and sugar. Beat together: eggs, milk and lemon rind. Pour this mix over the buttered bread in the bowl. Cover with plastic and leave in refrigerator for 2 hours. Sprinkle 1 tablespoon brown sugar and nutmeg on top and bake at 275° F for 50 minutes to 1 hour, until custard is set. Serves 4-6. Serve warm.

✿✿✿✿✿✿✿✿✿

Hot Potato Salad on a Bed of Spinach
Islands Pork Chops
Glazed Carrots
Cranberry Bread
Gingersnap Ice Cream Sandwiches

✧ ✧ ✧ ✧ ✧ ✧ ✧ ✧ ✧ ✧

HOT POTATO SALAD ON A BED OF SPINACH
(Prepare partially day before.)

6 medium all-purpose potatoes, scrubbed, boiled in jackets for about 20 minutes, drained;
    refrigerate (cover bowl in plastic) for 2 hours
$\frac{1}{2}$ cup chopped celery
$\frac{1}{2}$ cup chopped onion
1 small green sweet pepper, seeded, chopped
$\frac{1}{2}$ cup mayonnaise
2 tbsp. cider vinegar
$\frac{1}{2}$ tsp. salt
1 tsp. dill weed
$\frac{1}{4}$ tsp. black pepper
1 tsp. brown sugar
$\frac{1}{2}$ tsp. dry mustard
2x2-inch chunk of sharp cheddar, cubed
2 slices bacon, cooked, drained on paper towels
Hungarian paprika

On the day: preheat oven to 275° F. In a small bowl blend mayonnaise, vinegar, salt, dill weed, pepper, brown sugar and dry mustard. Set aside. Hand peel cold potatoes and cut them into small chunks, 1x1-inch. Cut cheese into tiny chunks $\frac{1}{4}$ -inch square.
Pour potatoes, celery, onion, green pepper into an oven-resistant casserole dish.
Crush bacon and add to mixture. Toss with 2 spoons to combine. Pour the dressing over the bowl and toss to mix. Sprinkle paprika (use Hungarian paprika for taste) on top and warm in oven at 275° F for 20-25 minutes. Spoon warm, on individual salad plates on a bed of spinach. Serves 6.

....

ISLANDS PORK CHOPS

4-6 loin pork chops, $\frac{3}{4}$-inch thick, trimmed of fat
2 tbsp. olive oil
1 onion, chopped
$\frac{1}{4}$ cup light rum
3-4 tbsp. soy sauce
1 cup chicken stock (use canned consommé or mash 1 chicken bouillon in 1 cup
    of hot water)
$\frac{1}{2}$ cup tomato catsup
$\frac{1}{2}$ tsp. black pepper
4 slices (1 small can) pineapple (save juice)
6 prunes, pitted
1 tsp. brown sugar

In a large heavy skillet with cover, cook onion for 1 minute, scraping pan; move onions to sides of pan. Add pork chops (you may have to cook them 2-3 at a time), spooning onions on top side of chops. Sauté chops on both sides until lightly browned. Remove chops with onions to platter. Discard any leftover fat in skillet. Pour rum into skillet and scrape off any onion and pork bits. Add soy sauce, catsup, pineapple juice, stock, brown sugar and pepper; bring to a low simmer as you stir to blend the ingredients. Return and fit the chops and onion back into the pan. Place the pineapple slices and prunes on top of chops. Cover and gently simmer until the chops are tender, about 20-25 minutes.
If sauce becomes too thick, add more stock, rum or water. Serves 4-6.

………………………………..

GLAZED CARROTS

4-6 carrots, pared, thinly sliced in rounds
$\frac{1}{4}$ cup honey
$\frac{1}{4}$ cup Dijon mustard
2 tbsp. chopped candied ginger
1 tbsp. olive oil
1 tbsp. chopped parsley

Steam carrots for 5 minutes; drain. Meanwhile, combine honey, mustard, candied ginger and oil in a small sauce pan and bring to a boil. Remove sauce from heat and stir into hot carrots. Sprinkle with parsley. Serves 4-6.

………………………………..

CRANBERRY BREAD
(Prepare day before.)

2 cups flour
1 cup sugar
1 $\frac{1}{2}$ tsp. baking powder
$\frac{1}{2}$ tsp. baking soda
1 tsp. salt
1 egg, beaten, or $\frac{1}{4}$ cup egg substitute
$\frac{3}{4}$ cup orange juice
1 tbsp. grated orange rind
3 tbsp. canola oil
$\frac{1}{2}$ cup walnuts or pecans, chopped
2 cups coarsely chopped cranberries (use food processor)

Preheat oven to 350° F. Grease one 5x7-inch baking loaf pan. Sift together in a large bowl: flour, sugar, baking powder, baking soda, and salt. In a small bowl, combine beaten egg, juice, rind and oil. Add this mixture to flour mix in large bowl. Mix only to dampen. Carefully fold in nuts and berries. Pour into prepared pan and bake in preheated oven at 350° F for 1 hour, or until inserted toothpick comes out clean.

…………………………..

GINGERSNAP ICE CREAM SANDWICHES
(Prepare cookies up to one week in advance. Store tightly in tin.)

3 cups flour
2 tsp. baking powder
1 tsp. cinnamon
2 tsp. ginger
$\frac{1}{2}$ tsp. ground cloves
$\frac{1}{4}$ tsp. salt
$\frac{1}{2}$ cup butter or Smart Balance spread, softened
1 large egg or $\frac{1}{4}$ cup egg substitute
$\frac{1}{4}$ cup molasses
$\frac{1}{2}$ cup granulated sugar (for tops of cookies)
1 pkg. (16 oz.) butterscotch morsels

Preheat oven to 375° F. Mix flour, baking soda, spices, salt. In a large bowl, beat butter and sugar. When creamy, beat in egg and molasses. Stir into flour mix, mixing well. Cover with plastic and chill in refrigerator for 1 hour.

Form dough into 2-inch balls and place on lightly greased cookie sheets, 1-2 inches apart. With back of teaspoon, press tops of cookies to flatten slightly. Dip tops of cookies into granulated sugar and place on cookie sheets. Bake for 8-10 minutes until just dry on tops of cookies. Cookies will be soft in the middle, and little cracks will form on tops. Remove from oven and transfer to racks to cool. You probably will use 3 baking sheets, 9x15-inches. These cookies should be about 3-inches in diameter. Store in airtight tins, in a dry, cool place. Yields about 3 dozen large cookies or 64 cookies, $1\frac{1}{2}$ inches in diameter.

On the day, slightly soften 1 quart vanilla ice cream. Gently spoon and flatten 1 tablespoon of ice cream onto the pan-side of one-half of the number of cookies. Pour butterscotch morsels into a wide bowl BEFORE you begin this procedure. WORK QUICKLY. Dip the cookie with the flattened ice cream into the bowl of morsels (ice cream side); then, place another gingersnap on top of ice cream with morsels. Voila! You've created a gingersnap ice cream sandwich! Place cookies on a tray and freeze for at least 1 hour prior to serving. Remove tray AT serving; serve from tray. It would be a good idea to lay a paper doily on the cookie tray before forming the sandwiches.
(Recipe for "Gingersnaps" appears in MENU LOG by Marion O. Celenza, page 384.)

✿✿✿✿✿✿✿✿✿✿

Green Beans, Carrots and Provolone Salad
Pasta in Chicken Ragout
Rum Raisin Frappe

✿✿✿✿✿✿✿✿✿

GREEN BEANS, CARROTS AND PROVOLONE SALAD

3 cups fresh green beans, trimmed, rinsed, drained, cut into pieces, steamed for
    5 minutes, drained
2 cups shredded carrots
½ lb. chunk extra sharp provolone cheese, cut into julienne strips
¼ cup chopped filberts (hazelnuts)
¼ cup chopped Italian parsley
¼ cup torn fresh basil leaves
2 garlic cloves, minced
Caesar Dressing (see page 175)

In a large salad bowl combine cooked beans, carrots, cheese strips, parsley, basil and nuts. Toss to mix. Sprinkle garlic over top. Cover with plastic and refrigerate. Prepare Caesar Dressing. At serving time, drizzle the dressing over the salad, toss and serve. Serves 4-5.

…………………………..

PASTA IN CHICKEN RAGOUT

3 tbsp. olive oil
2-3 chicken breasts, skinned, boned, cut into strips
1 large onion, sliced thin
1 large carrot, peeled and shredded
2 garlic cloves, minced
½ cup hot water
½ cup dry white wine
1 large can Italian plum tomatoes (about 3 cups)
1 tsp. each: dried oregano and rosemary
1 tbsp. torn basil leaves
1 tsp. salt
½ tsp. black pepper
few flakes of hot red pepper
2 cups broccoli florets
1 red pepper, seeded, sliced thin
4-5 small white mushrooms, rinsed, quartered
1 lb. fettuccine pasta (add 1 tbsp. olive oil when cooking to prevent sticking)

In a large heavy saucepot, heat oil on moderate, add chicken strips and sauté, turning frequently for 5 minutes until lightly browned. Add onion, garlic and carrots and sauté for 2 minutes. Add hot water to pot and scrape bottom of pot. Add wine, tomatoes, herbs, salt and pepper (and a few flakes of hot pepper). Cover and gently simmer for 10 minutes. Add and stir the broccoli, red pepper and mushrooms into the mix. Simmer for another 5 minutes. While you are preparing the sauce, prepare the pasta pot. Follow cooking directions for fettuccine and add olive oil to the boiling water. Cook the pasta al dente. Drain and pour into a very large bowl for serving. Add the chicken and vegetable mix to the pasta and toss to mix. Serve immediately in individual pasta bowls. Serves 6.

………………………………..

RUM RAISIN FRAPPE

2 or more large bananas, quartered lengthwise
$\frac{1}{2}$ cup golden raisins
1 cup red seedless grapes
$\frac{1}{4}$ cup rum
vanilla ice cream
caramel sauce
heavy whipping cream

Whip the cream; refrigerate. Soak the raisins in rum for 30 minutes. At serving time, arrange 2 strips of bananas on each frappe-style dessert dish, twice as long as it is wide, with a rim. Lay 2 scoops of ice cream on bananas. Strew the grapes around the ice cream balls. Spoon 2 tablespoons caramel sauce over ice cream and fruit. Add a spoonful or two of rum raisins and a dollop of whipped cream. Serves 4 or more.

✩✩✩✩✩✩✩✩✩

Lettuce and Tomato Salad with Ceci
Stuffed Fish Fillets with Crabmeat
Brownie Sundae

✿✿✿✿✿✿✿✿✿✿

LETTUCE AND TOMATO SALAD WITH CECI

1 head of iceberg lettuce, trimmed, rinsed and drained, cut into 4-6 wedges
2 tomatoes, each cut into 6 wedges
1 can (1 lb.) ceci, rinsed and drained
1 small red onion, chopped
2-3 garlic cloves, chopped
1 tbsp. oregano
$\frac{1}{2}$ cup sliced pimiento olives

Bleu Cheese Dressing (see page 175)

Arrange salad on individual salad plates. On each plate, place a lettuce wedge and tomato wedges adjacent to each other. Spoon olives over the lettuce. Add garlic, onion and oregano to ceci. Spoon the chick pea mix in-between lettuce and tomato. Prepare Bleu Cheese Dressing and pour a serving spoonful over each salad. Serves 4-6.

……………………………..

STUFFED FISH FILLETS WITH CRABMEAT

4-6 fish fillets (flounder or grey sole)

STUFFING:
2 cups crabmeat, free of membrane,
   chopped in small pieces
$\frac{1}{2}$ cup unseasoned bread crumbs
1 tbsp. chopped onion
1 tbsp. chopped parsley
$\frac{1}{4}$ tsp. salt
$\frac{1}{4}$ tsp. black pepper
2 tbsp. olive oil
2 tbsp. water
a dash of Tabasco sauce to taste

COATING:
$\frac{1}{2}$ cup flour
$\frac{1}{2}$ cup unseasoned crumbs
salt and pepper to taste
1 egg beaten with 1 tbsp. water or egg
   substitute

VEGETABLE ACCOMPANIMENT:
1 can (1 lb.) artichoke hearts, unseasoned, drained, halved
1 large red pepper, seeded, thinly sliced
1 cup shredded mozzarella
2 tbsp. olive oil
2 tbsp. balsamic vinegar
black pepper to taste
oil to coat pan
4-6 small metal skewers

Preheat oven to 425° F. Prepare the stuffing: in a small bowl, combine crabmeat, crumbs, onion, parsley, salt, pepper, olive oil and water. Mix thoroughly. Set aside. Prepare the vegetables and accompaniment: in a medium-size bowl combine sliced red pepper and artichokes. Toss with oil and vinegar, pepper and salt. Set aside.

Pour one-half cup flour on a sheet of waxed paper. Pour $\frac{1}{2}$ cup unseasoned crumbs on another sheet of waxed paper. Beat egg with water in a flat dish. Have a greased 9x12 pan (preferably non-stick) ready. Lay fillets, one at a time, on waxed paper with flour. Pat 2 tablespoons or more of crab stuffing on one-half of each fillet. Fold fish over and with your hands, dip each fillet into the beaten egg on both sides of the fold and then coat each fillet with the crumbs. Pinch the halves together with a skewer and lay the fillets in the greased pan. Surround the fish with the vegetable mix. Sprinkle mozzarella on fillets and vegetables. Roast in preheated oven 425° F for 15-20 minutes. Fish will start to lightly brown. Before serving, drizzle a little olive oil and balsamic vinegar and black pepper over the fish. Serves 4-6.

....

BROWNIE SUNDAE

2-3 brownies, crumbled in small chunks (prepare Brownies as below or use store-bought)
chocolate ice cream (or chocolate chip)
chocolate sauce: prepare by melting 3 oz. semi-sweet chocolate chips with 1 tbsp. butter
    in top part of small double boiler, stirring sauce as it melts over hot water (or use
    bottled chocolate sauce)
½ pt. raspberries, gently rinsed and drained; mash with fork in small bowl

Spoon 1-2 balls ice cream in sundae dessert glasses. Garnish with brownie crumbs; ladle sauce over ice cream and spoon raspberries over all. Serves 4-6.

The following recipe for "Brownies" comes from MENU LOG by Marion O. Celenza.

BROWNIES
½ cup granulated sugar
½ cup sifted flour
2 oz. melted Baker's chocolate
½ cup canola oil
4 eggs, beaten or 1 cup egg substitute
¼ cup chopped nuts
pinch of salt

Preheat oven to 350° F. In a double boiler, over hot water, melt chocolate blended with oil. Stir and set aside. In a 4-quart mixing bowl, beat eggs and sugar until creamy. Fold in chocolate-oil mix and add sifted flour with salt. Beat until smooth and stir in nuts. Spoon into well-greased baking pan, 8x8 inches. Spread batter evenly. Bake at 350° F about 35 to 45 minutes. Cool thoroughly before cutting.

✧✧✧✧✧✧✧✧✧

Antipasto, page 171

Almond Slices, page 7

Vineyard in the Snow, page 5

CINNAMON CHICKEN, PAGE 93   **PARMESAN CHICKEN, PAGE 4**

PEAR AND GORGONZOLA SALAD, PAGE 16   **COUPE SAINT-JACQUES, PAGE 73**

Three-Bean Salad and Pasta, page 28

Chicken Pot Pie, page 122

CRANBERRY BREAD, PAGE 114   **COBB SALAD WITH BEETS AND ONIONS, PAGE 72**

PASTA, WILD ALASKA SALMON AND CHEDDAR, PAGE 154

IRISH SODA BREAD, PAGE 38

CHICKEN FINGERS SALAD, PAGE 64

RUSTIC PASTA, PAGE 3

TRIFLE, PAGE 32

A BUNCH OF BRUNCHES

Chicken Pot Pie
Golden Apples

☕ ☕ ☕ ☕ ☕ ☕ ☕ ☕ ☕ ☕

CHICKEN POT PIE

PASTRY:
1 ½ cups flour
1 tsp. salt
⅓ cup chilled butter or Smart Balance spread, cut into small pieces
1 large egg beaten with 2-3 tbsp. ice water
(Glaze: 1 large egg, beaten or ¼ cup egg substitute)

In a medium bowl, mix together flour and salt. Using a pastry blender or 2 knives, cut butter into flour to form coarse crumbs. In a small bowl, beat together egg and water. Add to flour mix; knead lightly to form a soft dough. Shape into a disk; wrap in plastic; chill in refrigerator for 1 hour.

FILLING:
4 cups cooked chicken breasts, cubed; save stock
1 tbsp. olive oil
1 large onion, chopped
1 cup frozen peas
1 small carrot, pared, chopped
6 small mushrooms, cleaned, quartered
¼ cup dry white wine (or water)

1 can (13 ½ oz.) evaporated milk
2 tbsp. flour
1 ½ tsp. Hungarian paprika
1 tbsp. chopped dill
½ tsp. salt
½ tsp. black pepper
½ cup stock from cooked chicken

Simmer the chicken breasts. Set ½ cup stock aside. Cube the chicken and place in a 9x13-inch casserole dish (Pyrex or heat-resistant). In a skillet, melt 1 tablespoon butter and sauté mushrooms and onion until lightly brown, about 3 minutes; stir in peas and carrots; add the wine and cook for 2-3 minutes. Add mushroom mix to chicken in casserole; stir to combine. In a medium-size saucepot, whisk together: evaporated milk, flour, salt, pepper and paprika over low heat. Cook until thickened, about 5 minutes. Stir in stock and cook for 5 minutes. Pour sauce over chicken and vegetables and stir and fold to mix. Preheat oven to 400° F.

Lightly flour board and rolling pin. Roll out chilled dough to fit top of the casserole. Place on top of pie; trim and seal the edges. Prick a flower design into crust, for airholes. Beat egg (or substitute) and brush the glaze over the pastry. Bake in preheated oven 400° F until filling is bubbly and crust is golden brown, 25-30 minutes. Serve warm. Serves 4-6.

. . . .

GOLDEN APPLES

4-6 golden delicious apples, cored, cut off $\frac{1}{4}$-inch from tops of apples
1 can (6 oz.) apple juice
$\frac{1}{4}$ cup brown sugar
$\frac{1}{2}$ cup raisins
$\frac{1}{4}$ cup chopped walnuts
juice of 1 lemon
1 tbsp. lemon rind
1 tbsp. chopped candied ginger
1 tsp. butter to coat Pyrex casserole
vanilla ice cream

Preheat oven to 375° F. In a small bowl, combine apple juice, brown sugar, lemon juice, rind and ginger. Butter the bottom of a 9x13 Pyrex (or heat-resistant) casserole dish. Arrange the cored apples in the dish. Stuff the apples with raisins and nuts. Pour the liquid over the apples and bake at 375° F for 45-50 minutes or until skin starts to crack. Serve warm with a dollop of vanilla ice cream on top of apple. Serves 4-6.

French Toast Sandwiches with Cured Ham and Cranberries
Salad of Figs, Oranges and Apples
Autumn Rice Custard

FRENCH TOAST SANDWICHES WITH CURED HAM AND CRANBERRIES

8-10 thick slices whole wheat bread (or hearty whole grain bread)
4 eggs, beaten or egg substitute
$\frac{1}{4}$ cup low fat milk
2 cups crushed flake cereal (bran flakes, raisin bran, Wheaties) spread on board
4-5 thick slices or more ($\frac{1}{4}$-inch thick) cured ham
4-5 slices Jarlsberg Swiss Cheese
Dijon mustard spread
canola oil to coat skillet
1 pkg. (12 oz.) fresh cranberries
1 cup water
1 cup granulated sugar

Prepare the cranberry sauce the day before. (When cranberries are in season, store 2-3 packages in your freezer for future use.) In a 2-quart pot, combine cranberries, water and sugar. Stir to dissolve the sugar. Cover, bring to a boil; then simmer for 10 minutes, stirring occasionally. Remove from burner, cool and pour into container with cover. Refrigerate to gel.

On the day, lay out 4-5 slices of bread. Spread 1 teaspoon of mustard on each slice of bread. Lay a slice or two of ham on the bread, followed by a slice of cheese. Top with another slice of bread. In a wide-mouthed bowl, beat eggs with milk. Heat the oil in the skillet to moderately hot, 300° F. Dip both sides of each sandwich into the egg mix. Then, coat each sandwich on both sides with cereal crumbs. (Crush the cereal by spreading cereal on a board, covered with waxed paper; then, by working a rolling pin over the waxed paper.) Toast sandwiches in the skillet for 2 minutes on each side until lightly browned. With spatula, remove to heat-resistant serving platter. Lay a loose sheet of foil over platter and keep warm in low oven. Serve with a portion of cranberry sauce. Serves 4-5.

……………………………..

SALAD OF FIGS, ORANGES AND APPLES

Apple Cider Dressing (see page 177)
3 large navel oranges, skin peeled, sectioned, pith removed
8-10 fresh figs (in season) or use figs in a glass jar, quartered
2 apples, your choice, cored, each apple sliced into 8 wedges (leave skin)
$\frac{1}{2}$ cup roasted whole almonds with skin
1 tbsp. olive oil
1 tbsp. cinnamon

Prepare Apple Cider Dressing. Coat almonds with cinnamon and olive oil. Preheat oven to 450° F. Spread almonds on a sheet of foil. Roast them for 2-3 minutes at 450° F. In a large bowl combine orange sections, figs, almonds, apples and dressing. Stir to blend thoroughly. Chill for 1 hour. Serve in individual fruit bowls. Serves 4-5.

………………………………..

AUTUMN RICE CUSTARD

1 $\frac{1}{2}$ cups cooked white rice
$\frac{1}{2}$ cup golden raisins, soaked in 2 tbsp. rum for one hour
2 eggs or $\frac{1}{2}$ cup egg substitute
1 $\frac{1}{2}$ cups evaporated milk (fat-free may be used)
$\frac{1}{2}$ cup granulated sugar
1 sm. can (1 lb.) pure pumpkin
1 tsp. nutmeg
1 pt. heavy cream for whipping; added nutmeg

Preheat oven to 375° F. Blend rum-soaked raisins into cooked rice; pour into greased Pyrex dish (1 quart). Beat together: eggs, milk, sugar, pumpkin and nutmeg. Pour this mix over entire casserole of rice mix. Bake at 375° F for 45-50 minutes, or until tester removes clean. Cool. Decorate with dollops of whipped cream; sprinkle with added nutmeg. Serves 4-6.

Chicken and Spinach
Blueberry Muffins

CHICKEN AND SPINACH

4-6 thin-sliced chicken breasts, skinned, boned, cutlet-style, washed, patted dry with
    paper towels
1 cup fine corn flake crumbs
2 eggs, beaten, or $\frac{1}{2}$ cup egg substitute
$\frac{1}{4}$ cup low-fat milk
canola oil for sautéing
12–18 slices Portobello mushrooms
4 tbsp. olive oil,
2 tbsp. balsamic vinegar
2 large beefsteak tomatoes, thinly sliced in rounds
Cheddar Cheese Sauce (see page 179)
10 oz. baby spinach, rinsed and drained

Preheat broiler to 475° F. Prepare Cheddar Cheese Sauce. Coat mushroom slices with a mix of olive oil and balsamic vinegar; arrange on grill pan and broil at 475° F for 1-2 minutes on each side. Set aside. Heat the oil in a large skillet. Spread corn flake crumbs on a sheet of waxed paper. In a wide-mouthed bowl, beat eggs and milk. Dip chicken cutlets into egg mix and coat with crumbs. Sauté in a skillet for 4-5 minutes on each side. Transfer to warming platter. Prepare on individual plates: make a bed of spinach on each plate. Place a layer of 2-3 slices of tomato on spinach. Lay a warm chicken cutlet on the tomato and spinach. Next, place 3-4 slices of mushrooms and ladle a large spoonful of Cheddar Cheese Sauce over the plate. Serve warm. Serves 4-6.

....

BLUEBERRY MUFFINS
(Prepare day before)

Follow the directions for Cranberry Bread on page 114. Instead, use a pan for medium-size muffins. Grease the muffin cups. Substitute for cranberries: 2 cups blueberries, washed, drained. Spoon batter into the prepared muffin tin and bake at 350° F for 20-25 minutes or until inserted toothpick comes out clean. Make 5-6 muffins.

Ham Steak and Corn Fritters
Apples, Pears and Grapes in Wine
Butternut Squash Soup with Sausage

HAM STEAK AND CORN FRITTERS

4-5 ham steaks (about 6 oz. each)
4-5 round slices fresh pineapple (or 1 small can of pineapple slices)
1 small can apple juice (6 oz.)
2 tbsp. brown sugar
1 tsp. ground cinnamon
$\frac{1}{4}$ tsp. ground cloves
1 tsp. mustard powder

Preheat oven to 300° F. In a small bowl, blend apple juice, brown sugar, cinnamon, cloves and mustard powder. Lay ham steaks in 9x13 Pyrex, heat-resistant casserole dish. Lay a pineapple slice on each steak. Pour sauce over ham and bake, uncovered at 300° F for 20 minutes. Serves 4-5 (with corn fritters).

CORN FRITTERS

1 can (1 lb.) creamed corn
2 eggs or $\frac{1}{2}$ cup egg substitute, well beaten
1 cup Bisquick
1 tsp. baking powder
1 tsp. ground nutmeg
$\frac{1}{4}$ tsp. black pepper
$\frac{1}{2}$ tsp. salt
2-4 tbsp. canola oil for frying

In a medium-size bowl, beat eggs; add creamed corn; stir in flour, baking powder, nutmeg, salt and pepper. Make a fairly smooth thick batter. Preheat skillet to medium-high 300° F; pour enough canola oil in bottom of skillet to brown the fritters. Drop batter from large tablespoon into hot oil, making 3-4 fritters at a time. Turn over to brown other side. When cooked, transfer with spatula, to paper towels to drain. Arrange them on warm serving platter. Serves 4-5.

....

APPLES, PEARS AND GRAPES IN WINE

2-3 apples: Rome Beauty or Granny Smith, cored, skin removed, cut into chunks
2-3 Bosc pears, skin removed, cored, cut into chunks
2 cups seedless red grapes
1 tbsp. lemon juice
¼ cup brown sugar
¼ cup dry Sherry
¼ cup water

In a 2-quart saucepot, combine apples, pears, grapes, sugar, lemon juice, Sherry and water. Stir to mix. Bring to a boil, then simmer gently for 10 minutes or until apples and pears are just tender. Do not overcook. Remove from heat and transfer to serving bowl. Cool. May be served cool or warm in dessert bowls. Serves 4-5.

………………………………..

BUTTERNUT SQUASH SOUP WITH SAUSAGE

1 ½ cups chicken broth (or water)
1 cup vegetable stock
2 lbs. butternut squash (makes about 3
    cups when puréed)
1 ½ cups cubed potatoes
1 small onion, chopped
½ cup celery, chopped
1 carrot, peeled, chopped
2 tbsp. butter, or Smart Balance
    margarine
2 tbsp. flour

1 tbsp. chopped parsley (save additional
    2 tbsp. for garnish)
¼ tsp. black pepper, or to taste
1 ½ tsp. salt, or to taste
2 tbsp. brown sugar
1 tsp. cinnamon
1 tsp. ground ginger
½ cup crumbled sweet sausage meat
1 tbsp. olive oil
3 cups evaporated milk (you may use
    fat-free)

Brown sausage meat and onion in olive oil in a small skillet; set aside. Pare and cube butternut squash and place in 6-quart soup pot to which 1 ½ cups chicken broth has been added. Prepare potatoes, celery, carrot and add to the soup pot. Simmer the vegetables for 10 minutes; drain the vegetables and save the stock and add about 1 cup vegetable stock to soup pot. Transfer vegetables to food processor to purée. Pour the puréed vegetables into the soup pot; stir in the cooked sausage/onion mix. In a small bowl, blend flour into butter to form a smooth paste; stir in 3 cups evaporated milk, parsley, sugar, salt, pepper, cinnamon and ginger. Pour this mix into the soup pot, mixing thoroughly (a whisk will help you). Cook the soup, uncovered, to a low simmer for 30 minutes, stirring frequently. Garnish each portion with chopped parsley. Serves 4-6.

TORTA RUSTICA
(May be prepared several days in advance and refrigerated.)

2 lbs. ricotta
6 eggs, beaten or 1 ½ cups egg substitute
6 Italian sweet sausages grilled, sliced
   into narrow rounds
½ lb. mozzarella, shredded
½ lb. sharp provolone, diced

1 cup Parmesan cheese, grated
½ lb. Swiss cheese, diced
¼ tsp. black pepper
½ red pepper, diced
½ green pepper, diced

Preheat oven to 375° F. Grease a 9-inch spring-form pan. In a large mixing bowl, beat ricotta with beaten eggs and mix well. Stir in remaining ingredients and pour into a well-greased 9-inch spring-form pan. Bake at 375° F for 1 hour or until firm. Cool to room temperature. Run a knife around the edge of the pie before removing the sides. Serve at room temperature. Slice into serving wedges. Serves 6-8.

……………………………..

BERRY FRUIT WALDORF
(Chill fruits and vegetables before preparing.)

1 cup celery, diced
1 cup raspberries, gently rinsed and drained
1 cup blueberries, rinsed and drained
2 cups fresh pineapple cut into chunks; or use 1 small can (8 oz.) pineapple chunks
½ cup chopped pecans
3 cups salad greens: preferably chicory, romaine or green leaf (mix if desired)
1 cup mayonnaise
juice of 1 lemon
¼ tsp. black pepper

In a large salad bowl, mix celery, greens, berries, pineapple and pecans. In a small bowl, whip a smooth blend of mayo, lemon juice and pepper. Pour over salad, toss to mix. Serves 4-6.

Polenta with Sausages and Bacon
Tomato, Onion and Bacon Salad

POLENTA WITH SAUSAGES AND BACON
(Prepare sauce day before.)

1 cup fine cornmeal
$\frac{1}{2}$ cup cold water
4 cups boiling water
1 tsp. salt
$\frac{1}{4}$ tsp. black pepper
$\frac{1}{2}$ cup shredded sharp cheddar cheese
4 slices lean bacon
1 tbsp. olive oil
$\frac{1}{2}$ recipe: Mushroom Tomato Sauce (see page 184)
4-6 links sweet Italian sausage or chorizo
2 fennel bulbs, trimmed, sliced in rounds, $\frac{1}{4}$-inch thick
$\frac{1}{2}$ cup pitted olives, oil-cured
2 tbsp. olive oil

In a 2 $\frac{1}{2}$-quart pot with cover, blend $\frac{1}{2}$ cup cold water into 1 cup cornmeal. Bring 4 cups water to a boil and pour over cornmeal mix. Stir to mix thoroughly. Cover and cook on medium heat, stirring constantly for 20 minutes. Grease a large loaf pan and pour the mush into it. Cover with plastic and chill for 2 hours. Then, cook bacon in a skillet until crisp, not burnt. Remove bacon to paper towels. Drain off most of the bacon fat from skillet and scrape bottom of skillet; add 1 tablespoon olive oil. When the mush is firm, remove from refrigerator. Heat oil in skillet to medium-high; cut polenta into $\frac{1}{2}$-inch thick slices, and fry in skillet for a couple of minutes on each side. Arrange slices of polenta in a greased oven-proof casserole dish. In a clean skillet, preferably non-stick, brown sausage in 2 tablespoons olive oil until cooked thoroughly. In last few minutes, add sliced fennel and olives. Stir fennel and olives in pan with spatula. Transfer sausage mix to casserole with polenta slices. Dress the entire casserole with Mushroom Sauce mix, prepared in advance. Warm the sauce on burner. Now is the time to sprinkle the cheddar cheese and crumble the bacon on top of the sauce; heat in oven 350° F until cheese melts, about 15-20 minutes. Serves 4-6.

……………………………..

TOMATO, ONION AND BACON SALAD

1 large white onion, sliced in rounds, $\frac{1}{4}$-inch thick
6 plum tomatoes, quartered
6-8 basil leaves
1 tsp. dried oregano
2 garlic cloves, minced
2 strips bacon, cooked, drained, crumbled
2 tbsp. olive oil
black pepper, to taste

In a medium-size salad bowl, just before serving, combine tomatoes, onions, garlic, basil, oregano, black pepper. (Prepare bacon in advance.) Crumble bacon on top of salad and drizzle with olive oil. Serves 4-6.

Cheddar Cheese Soup
Poached Egg on Toast with Bacon
Tomato and Avocado Salad

CHEDDAR CHEESE SOUP

4 slices lean bacon, cooked until crisp,
    drained on paper towels
1 tbsp. olive oil
1 onion, finely chopped
2 stalks celery, finely chopped, include
    leaves
1 carrot, chopped fine
3 tbsp. flour

$\frac{1}{2}$ tsp. Hungarian paprika
4 cups chicken broth (canned consommé
    or mash 4 chicken bouillon cubes in
    4 cups boiling water)
1 cup evaporated milk
$\frac{3}{4}$ lb. grated, sharp cheddar cheese
3 tbsp. parsley, minced

Cook bacon until crisp. Set aside on paper towels. Remove bacon fat and scrape bottom of skillet: add 1 tablespoon olive oil. On moderate-low heat cook onion, celery and carrots for 8-10 minutes, until softened. Stir in flour and paprika and continue to cook and stir for 3 minutes. Stir in milk and cheese; cook over low heat stirring, until cheese is melted. Do not boil. Stir in parsley; garnish with crumbled bacon. Serves 4-6.

....

POACHED EGG ON TOAST WITH BACON

4-6 large slices bread, preferably whole grain
4-6 large eggs or egg substitute (1 cup - 1 $\frac{1}{2}$ cups)
dash of black pepper
4-6 slices cheddar cheese (available low-fat)
4-6 strips lean bacon. cooked crisp, drained on paper towel
greased cups for egg poacher

Cook bacon; set aside. Prepare a metal serving tray as you begin to poach the eggs. Poach 4-6 eggs over simmering water. Sprinkle eggs with black pepper. Toast the bread. Preheat oven to 400° F. Lay a slice of cheddar on toast; set a poached egg on top of cheese; lay a strip of bacon on top of egg. Heat at 400° F for a few minutes until cheese starts to melt. Serves 4-6.

....

TOMATO AND AVOCADO SALAD

large leaves Boston lettuce
2-3 large slicing tomatoes, sliced in rounds
2 medium-sized avocados, peeled, stone removed
1 red onion, thinly sliced
Russian Dressing (see page 174)

Prepare dressing in advance. Refrigerate. Prepare individual salad plates. Lay a large lettuce leaf on each plate. Add one slice or two of tomato on lettuce, followed by slices of avocado and some sliced onion. Drizzle 1-2 tablespoons of Russian Dressing over salad. Serves 4-6.

Sausage Pie
Very Berry

SAUSAGE PIE
(Start preparation night before.)

6-8 links Italian sausage with fennel seed, cooked, drained, cut into rounds
3 slices white bread, cubed (do not remove crusts)
1 cup grated sharp cheddar cheese
6 eggs or 1 ½ cups egg substitute, beaten
2 cups low-fat milk or fat-free evaporated milk
1 tbsp. dry mustard
salt, pepper to taste
olive oil to grease casserole

In a medium-size bowl, beat eggs and milk, mustard, salt and pepper and set aside.
In 9x12 heat-resistant greased casserole dish, layer cubed bread, sausage rounds
and cheese (in that order). Pour egg mix over casserole. Cover with plastic and
refrigerate, overnight. Then, bake in preheated oven, 350° F for 45 minutes.
Cut into squares; serves 4-5.

……………………………..

VERY BERRY

1 cup blueberries, rinsed, drained
1 cup raspberries, gently rinsed and drained
2 cups sliced strawberries (or a mixture of strawberries, blackberries, and pitted cherries)
½ cup cranberry juice
juice of 1 lemon, mint sprigs to garnish

In a dessert bowl arrange layers of 3-4 assorted berries. Blend cranberry juice with
lemon juice and drizzle over fruit bowl. Garnish with mint. Serves 4-6.

Salmon Stew
Fruits in Batter

SALMON STEW

1 ½ lbs. salmon fillet, skin removed, roasted, cubed
¼ cup honey mustard
2 tbsp. dill weed
2 ½ cups water
1 ½ cups evaporated milk
1-2 all-purpose potatoes, pared, cubed
1 small onion, chopped
½ pkg. (about 6 oz.) instant potato granules
1 tbsp. lemon juice
1 tsp. salt
½ tsp. black pepper
1 doz. 3-inch fresh asparagus tips, washed, drained
6 small white mushrooms, rinsed, thinly sliced
Hungarian paprika for garnish

Spread honey mustard on top side of skinned fillet. Sprinkle dill weed over fish. Roast in preheated oven at 375° F for 20-25 minutes. Meanwhile, on low to moderate heat, warm a mix of evaporated milk and water; add cubed potatoes and chopped onion. Cover and simmer for 5 minutes; add asparagus tips and mushrooms and continue to simmer for 10 minutes longer. Stir in the instant potato, a little at a time, making a thick broth. Stir in lemon juice, salt and pepper. Cube the roasted salmon (2x2-inches) and add to stew, stirring to mix. Simmer for another 10 minutes. Transfer to a soup tureen for serving. Sprinkle tureen of soup with Hungarian paprika. Serves 6.

....

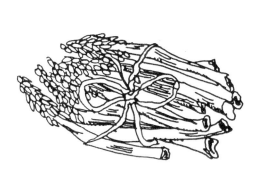

2 Granny Smith apples, peeled, cored, cut into small chunks
2 Bartlett or Bosc pears, peeled, cored, cut into chunks
1 cup pitted prunes
1 cup white raisins
$\frac{1}{2}$ cup butter or Smart Balance spread
1 cup brown sugar
1 $\frac{1}{4}$ cups Bisquick
$\frac{1}{2}$ cup low-fat milk
1 tbsp. brown sugar mixed with 1 tsp. ground cinnamon

Preheat oven to 325° F. In a 9-inch skillet with oven-proof handle, spread a blended mix of butter and brown sugar. Add apples, pears, pitted prunes and raisins. In a small bowl beat Bisquick with milk and spoon on top of fruit mix in skillet. Sprinkle with 1 tablespoon of brown sugar mixed with 1 teaspoon cinnamon. Bake in preheated oven 325° F for 30-35 minutes or until batter in golden and apples are tender. (Insert a metal skewer through apples to test for tenderness.) Serve warm. Serves 6.

Ham in a Crust
Bananas in Rum

࿙ ࿙ ࿙ ࿙ ࿙ ࿙ ࿙ ࿙ ࿙ ࿙
౿౿౿౿౿౿౿౿౿౿

HAM IN A CRUST

CRUST:
1 ½ cups flour
1 tsp. salt
⅓ cup chilled butter or Smart Balance spread, cut into small pieces
1 large egg, beaten with 2-3 tbsp. ice water, or ¼ cup egg substitute
1 egg beaten or ¼ cup egg substitute for glaze

In a medium bowl, mix together flour and salt. Using a pastry blender or 2 knives, cut butter into flour to form coarse crumbs. In a small bowl, beat together egg and water. Add to the flour mix and knead lightly to form a soft dough. Shape into a disk; cover in plastic wrap; chill in refrigerator for 1 hour.

FILLING:
2 sweet potatoes, pared, cut into small chunks
2 all-purpose potatoes, pared, cut into small chunks
3 cups cured ham, cut into julienne strips
2 tbsp. olive oil
½ red pepper, diced
½ green pepper, diced
1 large onion, chopped

3-4 small white mushrooms, chopped
1 can (13 ½ oz.) evaporated milk
2 tbsp. flour
1 tsp. salt
1 tsp. dry mustard
½ tsp. black pepper
½ cup water (from potatoes)
½ cup chopped pitted green olives

Cook the sweet potatoes and potatoes in boiling water for 5 minutes. Drain all but ½ cup of liquid and set aside. Sauté mushrooms and onions and peppers in oil in small pan. Grease a 9x15-inch Pyrex casserole (oven-proof) with a little oil. Arrange the julienne-cut ham on bottom of casserole. Add mushroom mix to ham. Sprinkle olives over mix. In a medium saucepan, whisk together: evaporated milk, flour, salt, pepper and mustard. Cook until thickened; slowly beat in potato water and cook for another 5 minutes. Pour sauce over ham and vegetables and stir and fold to mix.

Preheat oven to 400° F. Lightly flour board and rolling pin. Roll out chilled dough to fit top of the casserole. Place crust on top of casserole; trim and seal the edges. Prick the crust in several places with a fork to create air holes. Beat egg and brush the glaze over the crust. Bake in preheated oven 400° F for 25-30 minutes, until filling is bubbly and crust has browned. Serve warm. Serves 4-6.

....

BANANAS IN RUM

4 bananas (1 per serving), each peeled, cut lengthwise in 2-4 strips
1 tbsp. butter or Smart Balance spread for each serving
1 cup seedless red grapes
1 tbsp. brown sugar
1 tbsp. candied ginger
1 tbsp. lemon juice
$\frac{1}{4}$ cup dark rum
2 peeled and sliced kiwi for garnish

Serve in individual frappe dessert dishes.

Melt butter in a skillet and gently sauté bananas, a few strips at a time, first one side, then the other. Remove to dessert dishes as you cook. Add grapes to each serving. In a small pot, blend rum, lemon juice, brown sugar, candied ginger and simmer for 1-2 minutes. Spoon over bananas and grapes. Garnish with kiwi slices. Serves 4.

Prosciutto and Cheese Quiche
Chef's Salad

❧ ❧ ❧ ❧ ❧ ❧ ❧ ❧ ❧
☕☕☕☕☕☕☕☕☕

PROSCIUTTO AND CHEESE QUICHE

CRUST:
1 $\frac{1}{3}$ cups flour
$\frac{1}{8}$ tsp. salt
$\frac{1}{2}$ cup (1 stick) chilled butter, cut into small pieces
2-3 tbsp. cold water

FILLING:
10 strips prosciutto
4 large eggs or 1 cup egg substitute
1 $\frac{1}{2}$ cups evaporated milk
$\frac{1}{8}$ tsp. thyme
$\frac{1}{8}$ tsp. black pepper
$\frac{1}{2}$ cup Swiss cheese, shredded
$\frac{1}{2}$ cup cheddar cheese, shredded

Prepare the crust. Have ready, a 9-inch pie pan. In a large bowl, mix flour with salt.
Using a pastry blender or 2 knives, cut in the butter until coarse crumbs form. Add water,
1 tablespoon at a time, tossing with a fork, until a dough forms. Knead gently and form
dough into a disk; cover in plastic wrap and chill in refrigerator for 30 minutes. Preheat
oven to 375° F. On a lightly floured board (and floured rolling pin) roll chilled dough
into an 11-inch circle. Fit into a 9-inch pie pan. Trim edge, leaving a $\frac{1}{4}$ -inch overhang.
Fold dough under to form a stand-up edge. Prick dough with fork in several places at
bottom and sides of pan. Line crust in pan with a sheet of foil and fill with pie weights
(or dried beans). Bake at 375° F for 10 minutes. Remove foil and weights. Continue to
bake for 5 minutes, until lightly golden. Remove from oven and cool.
Do not turn off oven.

Prepare the filling. Sauté the prosciutto slices in a skillet over medium heat for
6-8 minutes, until crisp. Transfer to paper towels to drain. In a medium-size bowl,
whisk together: eggs, evaporated milk, thyme and pepper. Pour into crust. Crumble
prosciutto and sprinkle over egg mix. Sprinkle cheese on top, spreading evenly. Bake at
375° F for 30 minutes or until golden and custard is set. Serve warm. Serves 5-6
generously. (You may wish to use ready-prepared crusts. I prefer refrigerated packaged
crusts, folded and wrapped in plastic. Follow directions to suit the recipe you are using.)

....

CHEF'S SALAD

2 cups greenleaf lettuce, rinsed, drained
3 cups baby spinach, rinsed, drained
1 cucumber, peeled, sliced in rounds
3-4 scallions, trimmed, minced
1 cup Swiss cheese cut into small cubes
2 hard boiled eggs, quartered
black pepper
French Dressing (see page 174)

Prepare French Dressing. Refrigerate until needed. In a large salad bowl mix greens and cucumber and scallions; add Swiss cheese and toss to mix. Shell and quarter eggs. Refrigerate. At serving, pour dressing on salad and toss to mix. Garnish egg wedges around the edge of the bowl and sprinkle black pepper on eggs. Serves 4-6.

Wheat Pasta, Bacon and Vegetables
Orange Ambrosia

WHEAT PASTA, BACON AND VEGETABLES

8 oz. whole wheat linguine pasta
1 can (1 lb.) ceci, rinsed and drained
$\frac{1}{4}$ cup olive oil
2 tbsp. white wine vinegar
2 tbsp. lemon juice
$\frac{1}{2}$ tsp. salt
1 tsp. oregano
1 bay leaf
4 garlic cloves, chopped
2-3 cups broccoli rabe (rapini) or broccoli florets, trimmed, washed, drained
4 small white mushrooms, rinsed, quartered
4 strips bacon, cooked crisp, drained on paper towels, set aside
$\frac{1}{2}$ cup Parmesan cheese, grated
1 large carrot, shredded
fresh basil leaves for garnish

Sauté broccoli rabe (or broccoli florets), mushrooms, ceci and garlic in $\frac{1}{4}$ cup olive oil, on low-moderate heat for 4-5 minutes. While continuing to stir add the vinegar, lemon juice, salt, and herbs. Simmer for another 2-3 minutes. Turn off skillet and set aside. Meanwhile prepare whole wheat linguine according to directions on package, cooking pasta al dente. Drain, saving about $\frac{1}{4}$ cup hot pasta water to add with pasta in serving bowl. Transfer pasta to a large serving bowl; pour in the sautéed broccoli rabe mix including all of the sauce. Toss to mix thoroughly. Sprinkle pasta with grated Parmesan and toss to mix. Spread shredded carrots over top of casserole and dress with 4 strips of cooked bacon. Serves 4-6 generously.

....

4-6 cold Honeybell oranges (in season, January and February;
    or California eating oranges)
½ cup dried cranberries
½ cup flaked coconut
2 kiwis, peeled, sliced into rounds
1 tbsp. honey
¼ cup sweet wine (Sherry or Marsala)
juice of 1 lemon
1 tsp. lemon rind

In a small bowl, combine wine, honey, lemon juice and rind; stir to mix. Remove peel from oranges and separate sections, halfway, as a blooming flower; place each orange into individual dessert bowls; spoon sauce into each orange cavity; garnish with coconut and slices of kiwi. Serves 4-6.

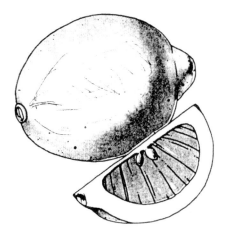

LITE-BITES FOR TWO

SHRIMP STUFFED MUSHROOMS
(May be prepared ahead of time and reheated.)

6-8 large stuffing mushrooms, scrubbed, remove stems and use in stuffing
6-8 whole extra-large shrimps, shelled, cleaned
1 cup plain Italian bread crumbs
¼ cup fresh parsley, chopped
mushrooms stems, cleaned, chopped
3 garlic cloves, peeled, minced
¼ tsp. freshly ground black pepper
dash of salt
dash of Tabasco sauce
¼ cup olive oil
½ cup grated extra-sharp provolone cheese
Hungarian paprika

Preheat oven to 375° F. Have ready: large round Pyrex baking plate, coated
with olive oil. In a 1-quart bowl, mix crumbs, chopped parsley, chopped
stems, minced garlic, black pepper, salt, Tabasco sauce, grated provolone and
olive oil. Add 1-2 tablespoons hot water (or dry vermouth) if stuffing is too
dry. Generously pack the mushrooms with this mix. Place in Pyrex dish and
press one cleaned shrimp into each filled mushroom cap. Sprinkle with
paprika. You may wish to drizzle a few drops of olive oil on each mushroom.
Bake mushrooms at 375° F for 20 minutes. As a luncheon accompaniment,
prepare one of the delicious salads from LUNCH IS IN THE BAG! while the
mushrooms are baking (or prepare salad in advance and refrigerate). Artisan
olive bread makes a tasty addition for this "brunch for two".

....

BASIC CROSTATA CRUST

1 lb. portion ready-to-use pizza dough (sold in supermarkets and bakeries)
½ cup finely grated Parmesan cheese
oil for greasing 12-inch pizza pan

If dough has been frozen, soften to room temperature. Place ball of dough (or dough section) in bowl coated with olive oil for 2 hours. Turn dough once. Then, stretch dough over a lightly oiled 12-inch pizza pan. Form a slightly raised dough rim around the edge of the pan. The dough should be about ½-inch thick. Sprinkle finely grated Parmesan cheese over the dough in the pan. Bake crust in preheated oven, 375° F for 10 minutes. Remove from oven and proceed as directed for individual Crostata recipes (which follow).

Arrange topping ingredients over the prepared crust, covering the crust up to the edge. Return to oven just before serving, and bake for another 12-13 minutes at 375° F. Do not over cook. Slice into 4-6 wedges. Serve hot with a small greens salad (see: Salads). Serves 2.

....

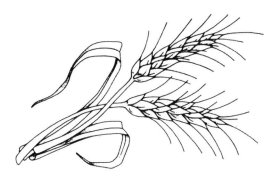

1 12-inch par-baked crostata (page 145)
1 red pepper, washed, cored, sliced thin
1 green pepper, washed, cored, sliced thin
4-6 white mushrooms, washed, sliced
1 can (1 lb.) whole artichoke hearts in water, drained, quartered
8-10 extra large shrimp, peeled, cleaned, simmered for 4-5 minutes, drained
¼ cup lemon juice
3-4 garlic cloves, minced
1 small yellow onion, sliced thin
¼ cup chopped pitted Sicilian olives
1 tbsp. dry oregano
2 tbsp. olive oil
1 tbsp. balsamic vinegar
freshly ground black pepper to taste
¼ cup grated Romano cheese

Arrange slices of red and green peppers over par-baked crust. Add sliced mushrooms and artichoke hearts. Dip each shrimp into lemon juice and set on top of vegetables. Sprinkle with olives, onions and garlic and oregano/black pepper and cheese. Drizzle olive oil and vinegar over entire crostata. Bake at 375° F as directed in crust recipe (page 145). Cut into wedges. Serve hot with Tomato and Avocado Salad (page 133).
Serves 2.

………………………………..

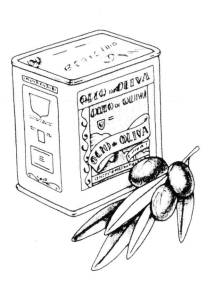

CROSTATA WITH PROVOLONE CHEESE, SALAMI AND VEGETABLES

1 12-inch par-baked crostata (see page 145)
½ red pepper, seeded, sliced thin
½ green pepper, seeded, sliced thin
½ yellow (or orange) pepper, seeded, sliced thin
4-6 small baby bella mushrooms, scrubbed, sliced
4-6 fresh plum tomatoes, cut into rounds
½ red onion, thinly sliced
3-4 garlic cloves, minced
½ cup pitted, chopped Sicilian and Greek olives
4 leaves fresh basil, torn into pieces
1 tbsp. dried oregano
cracked black pepper to taste
1 cup shredded slices Genoa Salami (about 4-5 slices)
2 tbsp. olive oil
½ cup sharp Provolone cheese, shredded

Arrange slices of red, green and yellow peppers over par-baked crust.
Add mushroom slices, tomato rounds, red onion and garlic. Spread olives
over crostata; sprinkle with basil leaves, oregano and cracked pepper.
Cover top with shredded salami and shredded provolone. Sprinkle olive oil
over entire crostata and bake at 375° F as directed in crust recipe
(page 145). Cut into wedges; serve hot with a small greens salad from
LUNCH IS IN THE BAG!. Serves 2.

....

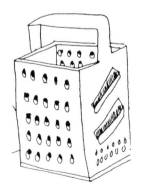

SICILIAN CROSTATA

1 12-inch par-baked crostata (page 145)
1 cup fresh or canned chopped plum tomatoes
6-8 small white mushrooms, chopped
1 small yellow onion, thinly sliced
4-6 garlic cloves, minced
1 can (2 oz.) flat anchovies in olive oil
2 tbsp. capers
½ cup oil-cured black olives, pitted
freshly ground black pepper
pinch of hot red pepper flakes
1 tbsp. dried rosemary
½ cup grated Parmesan cheese
½ cup shredded mozzarella cheese
2 tbsp. olive oil

Spoon plum tomatoes over par-baked crust. Scatter mushrooms, onion and garlic. Arrange anchovies over the crust and sprinkle the capers and olives to cover. Season with ground pepper and pepper flakes and rosemary. Scatter Parmesan and mozzarella cheeses over entire crostata and sprinkle with olive oil. Bake at 375° F as directed in crust recipe (page 145). Cut into wedges. Serve hot with a small greens salad (see salad recipes in LUNCH IS IN THE BAG!). Serves 2.

....

4-CHEESE CROSTATA WITH PEA SOUP

1 12-inch par-baked crostata (page 145)
1 cup shredded mozzarella (try smoky mozzarella for more flavor)
$\frac{1}{2}$ cup grated Parmesan cheese
$\frac{1}{2}$ cup grated Romano cheese
$\frac{1}{2}$ cup grated Asiago cheese
2 medium-size sweet red peppers, sliced thin
6 garlic cloves, chopped
1 cup pitted kalamata olives, chopped coarsely
freshly ground black pepper
2 tbsp. olive oil

Spread all of the cheeses over the par-baked crust. Arrange red pepper slices over the cheese. Scatter olives and garlic on top; sprinkle with black pepper and olive oil. Bake at 375° F as directed in crust recipe (page 145). Cut into wedges. Serve hot with PEA SOUP (follows). Serves 2.

PEA SOUP

4 cups boiling water into which 4 chicken bouillon cubes have been mashed
   (or 2 cups chicken broth-less salt variety, and 2 cups water)
1 pkg. (1 lb.) frozen peas
1 carrot, pared, chopped
1 large celery stalk, pared, chopped fine
1 small yellow onion, chopped fine
2 garlic cloves, minced
2 tbsp. olive oil
2-3 bay leaves (leave whole and remove before serving)
1 tbsp. dried oregano
freshly ground black pepper and salt to taste

Lightly brown onion and garlic in olive oil in 4-quart soup pot. Scrape bottom of pot; add hot chicken broth and stir to mix. Add peas, carrots, celery, bay leaves, oregano, salt and pepper. Bring pot to a boil; then, simmer covered for 35 minutes. Serves 3. (To try at another time: brown 2 slices lean bacon while you brown onions and garlic; crush the bacon and add to the mix.)

....

CROSTATA OF TOMATO, BROCCOLI AND PROSCIUTTO

1 12-inch par-baked crostata (page 145)
6 fresh plum tomatoes, thinly sliced wedges
1 dozen small broccoli florets, marinated for $\frac{1}{2}$ hour in 2 tbsp. balsamic
    vinegar and 2 tbsp. olive oil
1 small white onion, thinly sliced
4 garlic cloves, minced
1 cup shredded, thinly shaved prosciutto
$\frac{1}{2}$ cup mozzarella, small chunks
1 tbsp. dried oregano
2-3 torn leaves fresh basil
freshly ground black pepper to taste

Arrange plum tomatoes, drained broccoli (save the marinade), onion and
garlic over the par-baked crust. Spread prosciutto and mozzarella over the
vegetables. Sprinkle with herbs and black pepper and drizzle vinegar/oil
(the marinade) over entire crostata. Bake at 375° F as directed in crust
recipe (page 145). Cut into wedges; serve hot with Arugula, Radicchio and
Endive Salad (page 93). Serves 2.

....

SAUSAGE AND TOMATO CROSTATA

1 12-inch par-baked crostata (page 145)
2 cups prepared marinara sauce
2 sweet sausages with fennel, remove casing and finely chop
    the sausage meat
1 cup grated Parmesan cheese
1 small onion chopped
3-4 garlic cloves, minced
2 tbsp. olive oil
3-4 leaves fresh basil, chopped
1 tbsp. dried oregano
black pepper, salt to taste
1 small chile pepper, seeded, minced (Wear plastic gloves when working with
    hot pepper.)

Brown chopped sausage meat, onion and garlic in 2 tablespoons of olive oil.
Stir in chile pepper. Stir in marinara sauce, basil, oregano, salt and pepper.
Pour over par-baked crust. Generously sprinkle with cheese and bake at
375° F as directed in crust recipe (page 145). Serve hot. Cut into wedges.
Serve with Fennel Salad (page 13) or another Italian-style salad. Serves 2.

....

PEPPERONI AND GORGONZOLA CROSTATA

1 12-inch par-baked crostata (page 145)
2 sweet red peppers, thinly sliced
8 large pepperoni slices
2 cups thinly sliced yellow onion
2 tbsp. olive oil
2 tbsp. sweet butter (or Smart Balance spread)
1 ½ cups gorgonzola cheese, crumbled
6 fresh basil leaves, torn into small pieces
freshly ground black pepper, to taste

Arrange sliced red peppers and pepperoni slices over the par-baked crostata. In a small skillet, heat olive oil and butter; cook onions in this blend at 320° F, stirring constantly, until onions are caramel in color. Spread onions in sauce over peppers on crostata. Add crumbled gorgonzola, basil and black pepper across the entire crostata. Bake at 375° F as directed in crust recipe (page 145). Serve hot; cut into wedges and serve with a greens salad of your choice from LUNCH IS IN THE BAG! Serves 2.

…………………………………..

APPLE, WALNUTS AND CHEDDAR CROSTATA

1 12-inch par-baked crostata (page 145)
2 large Granny Smith apples, washed, cored, thinly sliced in rounds
½ cup brown sugar mixed with 1 tbsp. cinnamon
½ cup chopped walnuts
½ cup dried cranberries
¾ cup sharp cheddar cheese, crumbled
2 tbsp. butter or Smart Balance spread

Blend brown sugar/cinnamon on a large flat plate. Coat apple slices with this mix and arrange apples over the crostata. Pour the walnuts into the sugar mix and toss; then, spread sugared nuts over the coated apples. Scatter dried cranberries over crostata. Top with crumbled cheddar and dot with butter. Bake at 375° F as directed in crust recipe (page 145). Serve warm with Three Bean Salad (page 28). Serves 2.

…………………………………..

HAPPY DAY PANCAKES
(May be prepared in advance; stack with waxed paper between; package in foil and freeze until needed.)

4 cups Bisquick (low fat available)
2 eggs (or 2 portions egg substitute)
2 cups skim or non-fat evaporated milk (or use regular milk)

Additions:
1) 1 cup cranberries, rinsed, drained, chopped in food processor;
    2 tbsp. sugar
2) 2 cups chopped apples, pared and seeded; (coat with 2 tbsp, brown sugar,
    1 tbsp. cinnamon, 1 tbsp. lemon juice); ½ cup shredded, packaged low fat
    honey baked ham

canola oil for skillet (or griddle)
honey or maple syrup

Prepare basic batter. In a large bowl add 2 beaten eggs and 2 cups milk to 4 cups Bisquick. Beat to a smooth consistency. Pour half of the batter into another bowl and stir the cranberry-sugar mix. Set aside. To the remaining batter, add and mix: coated chopped apples and shredded ham.

Preheat pan to 320° F. Brush or coat the pan (griddle) with oil. Depending on size of pancake, pour ¼-½ cup of batter on griddle for each portion. Flip pancake and bake on both sides until light brown. May be frozen in stacks, as directed above. Heat thoroughly before serving (wrap short stacks in foil- no separation needed- in low oven 250° F). This recipe makes 10-15 pancakes, depending on size.

Each serving portion: 2-3 pancakes. (Save leftover pancakes in refrigerator or freezer.) Suggestions for this "Lite-Lunch": a bowl of Corn and Tomato Chowder (page 87) will make a delicious appetizer; Fresh Fruits in Ginger Sauce (page 51) is a tasty accompaniment.
Serves 2, with leftovers.

....

VEGETABLE MEDLEY

2 cups fresh green beans, trimmed, washed, drained, leave whole
¼ cup sliced almonds, with skin
1 can (1 lb.) black beans, rinsed, drained
1 sweet red pepper, seeded, sliced thin
1 tbsp. dried oregano, 2 garlic cloves, minced
3 medium-large carrots, pared, each cut into 4 thick sticks
3-4 tbsp. fresh chopped parsley
3-5 small Red Bliss potatoes, scrubbed, quartered, do not pare
1 small red onion, finely chopped
freshly ground black pepper, to taste
3 hard boiled eggs, shelled; slice each egg into 4 vertical cuts
Hungarian paprika

Honey Mustard Dressing (see page 173)

Have ready: a large platter or tray 9X15. Prepare Honey Mustard Dressing in advance. In a large vegetable steamer, with basket, arrange whole green beans, carrots, quartered potatoes. Add 1 cup hot water. Steam and simmer for 5 minutes. Meanwhile, pour beans into a small pot and top with red pepper slices and onions. Heat through at low temperature for 3-4 minutes. Remove basket from steamer and transfer vegetables to serving tray. Arrange the vegetables into horizontal sections: first, green beans; followed by carrots, potatoes and black beans/red pepper slices (from small pot). Sprinkle almonds over the green beans; top potatoes with chopped onion and 2 tablespoons chopped parsley; sprinkle 1 tablespoon parsley over carrots; arrange red pepper strips over black beans and sprinkle with garlic and oregano. Arrange quartered eggs around platter; sprinkle eggs with paprika; sprinkle the entire platter with freshly ground pepper. Shake dressing bottle vigorously and generously drizzle Honey Mustard Dressing over entire platter. Serve warm. Serves 2-3.
Pumpernickel Raisin bread is a fine accompaniment.

…………………………..

PASTA, WILD ALASKA SALMON AND CHEDDAR

$\frac{1}{2}$ lb. tri-color rotini pasta
1 can (1 lb.) wild Alaska pink salmon, drained, remove any skin and large bones
1 dozen small broccoli florets, washed, drained
$\frac{1}{2}$ sweet red pepper, seeded, sliced thin
$\frac{1}{2}$ cup sharp cheddar, small chunks
plain bread crumbs
Hungarian paprika (optional)

1 recipe Cheese Sauce (see page 179)

Prepare Cheese Sauce. Par-boil pasta in boiling water for
2-3 minutes less than directions on pasta package; drain and transfer to
large serving heat-resistant casserole dish (or bowl). Add broccoli, red
pepper and cheddar chunks. Pour cheese sauce over the pasta mix and
toss to coat. Sprinkle generously with bread crumbs (and paprika).
Bake in pre-heated oven, 350° F for 20 minutes. Serves 2, generously.
Suggested accompaniment: Allspice Pears (page 42).

....

VARIATIONS ON THE SCHNITZEL
(Advance preparation: Red Cabbage, Radishes, Cucumber and Tomato Salad,
    page 26)

2 slices cured ham, $\frac{1}{4}$-inch thick
2 large veal cutlets, pounded thin (cutlets should be about 4x6 inches
    in size)
2 tbsp. spicy mustard spread
1 tbsp. prepared horseradish
black pepper, to taste
2 eggs, fried (or poached; if poaching, use egg poacher-water under greased
    cups or rings)
2 tsp. capers
Hungarian paprika
canola oil to coat skillet; butter or Smart Balance spread

$\frac{1}{2}$ recipe: Red Cabbage, Radishes, Cucumber and Tomato Salad (page 26)

Heat oil in skillet to 320° F. Lay pounded cutlets on a sheet of waxed paper.
Spread each with 1 tablespoon mustard and $\frac{1}{2}$ tablespoon horseradish;
sprinkle with black pepper. Lay one slice of ham on each dressed cutlet.
When skillet temperature reaches 320° F, lay both "cutlet sandwiches" in
the skillet and cook for 2-3 minutes; with 2 spatulas, turn them over, ham-
side down and cook for another 1-2 minutes. Transfer (cutlet-side down) to
warming platter. (You may have to coat skillet again; this time use butter.)
Break 2 eggs over greased skillet and cook just until egg whites are firm.
Sprinkle eggs with capers and paprika. With spatula, remove each fried egg
to tops of cutlet sandwiches. Serve stacks on individual plates, accompanied
by a serving of Red Cabbage, Radishes, Cucumber and Tomato Salad (page 26).
Onion rye bread (with seeds) goes well with this recipe. Serves 2.

VARIATIONS of this recipe:
1) Substitute pork cutlets, instead of veal cutlets; follow recipe above.

2) Cook 4 slices bacon; drain. Set aside. Lay 2 slices calves liver on waxed
paper; spread each slice of liver with 1 tablespoon chopped onion, black
pepper and lay one bay leaf on top. Cook liver with topping in hot bacon
greased skillet, 320° F for 2-3 minutes; turn over once and cook for another
1-2 minutes; turn over again and transfer to serving plates. Remove bay
leaves and discard. Top with cooked bacon; top with cooked eggs.
(Advisement: high cholesterol/high fat content.)

....

SANDWICHES

A SCORE AND MORE

TOMATO, BACON AND PEANUT BUTTER ON WHOLE WHEAT TOAST

1 slice toasted whole wheat bread, spread with
2 tbsp. creamy peanut butter
3 strips cooked bacon, drained on paper towels
3 slices tomato, thinly cut; green leaf lettuce
top with 1 slice toasted whole wheat bread, spread with 1 tbsp. mayonnaise

....

CORNED BEEF SANDWICH

$\frac{1}{2}$-inch thick slice of cornbread with seeds; spread with
1 tbsp. spicy mustard
4 thin slices corned beef
2 thin slices Alpine Lace Swiss cheese; top with
$\frac{1}{2}$-inch thick slice of cornbread with seeds, spread with
1 tbsp. spicy mustard

Grill on both sides; cheese melts. Serve with Kosher garlic pickle.

....

TUNA MELT ON A ROLL

2 large Kaiser rolls, split

    Make a mix with:
1 can solid albacore tuna
$\frac{1}{2}$ cup chopped onion
$\frac{1}{2}$ cup chopped celery
2 tbsp. mayonnaise; spread tuna mix onto $\frac{1}{2}$ of Kaiser roll;

    on the other half, lay
2 slices Muenster cheese

Grill the open-face sandwiches; place a large leaf of greenleaf lettuce
between; close and serve. (Makes 2 open-face rolls.)

....

TURKEY, SMOKED HAM AND SWISS IN A PITA

large whole wheat pita, split

stuff with:
1 slice, $\frac{1}{4}$-inch thick turkey breast, spread with 2 tbsp. cooked cranberries,
1 slice Virginia ham, spread with spicy mustard,
1 slice Swiss cheese, spread with mayonnaise,
3 slices tomato
red leaf lettuce

(Or use 2 slices of potato bread, toasted, with whole cranberry sauce on side.)

....

EGG SALAD SANDWICH

2 slices whole wheat bread, or 1 large whole wheat pita, split

    Fill with of mix of:
1 hard cooked egg, mashed; stir in
2 tbsp. mayonnaise
$\frac{1}{4}$ cup chopped celery
$\frac{1}{4}$ cup chopped sweet pickles
1-2 slices tomato
greenleaf lettuce

Spread additional mayonnaise on bread.

....

WALDORF CHICKEN SALAD SANDWICH

1 slice pumpernickel raisin, spread with mayonnaise
    mix together:
$\frac{1}{2}$ cup cooked, boneless chicken, cubed
$\frac{1}{4}$ cup each: chopped apples, chopped celery
1 tsp. lemon juice, stirred into
2 tbsp. mayonnaise

Spoon salad onto pumpernickel raisin; top with greenleaf lettuce; top with another slice of pumpernickel raisin.
Serve with a portion of whole cranberry sauce (see page 124).

....

HAM AND CHEESE ON RYE

2 thick slices rye bread with seeds, spread with 1 tbsp. Dijon mustard

Fill with:
1 ($\frac{1}{4}$ -inch) slice honey-baked ham
1 ($\frac{1}{4}$ -inch) slice cheddar cheese
greenleaf lettuce

Accompany with a Kosher garlic pickle.

………………………………..

LIVERWURST ON PUMPERNICKEL

2 thick slices pumpernickel bread, spread with spicy mustard

Fill with:
3-4 slices Mother Goose liverwurst
1-2 thin slices red onion
greenleaf lettuce

………………………………..

HAM AND SWISS ON FRENCH TOAST

2 slices French Toast prepared as follows:
　　2 large slices white bread
　　1 egg, beaten, or egg substitute
　　2 tbsp. milk
　　2 tbsp. butter or Smart Balance or olive oil

Melt butter in skillet; dip bread into egg/milk mixture and cook in skillet on both sides until lightly browned.

On 1 slice French toast, lay:
　　1 slice Virginia ham
　　1 slice Alpine Lace Swiss

Spread 1 tbsp. mild mustard on second slice of French toast and form a sandwich. Return to skillet and grill 1 minute on each side (for cheese to melt).

………………………………..

FLAKY FRENCH TOAST WITH BACON

Prepare 2 thick slices whole wheat bread, dipped into 1 beaten egg (or egg substitute) and coated with crushed bran flakes or Raisin Bran flakes. Sauté on each side in 2 tbsp. butter or Smart Balance or olive oil. OR, bake on greased cookie sheet at preheated oven 450° F for 10 minutes.

Cook 3 slices bacon; drain on paper towels. Make a sandwich with bran flakes, French toast and bacon. Serve with ½ cup sliced strawberries or ½ cup blueberries.

....

PEANUT BUTTER AND BANANA ON PUMPERNICKEL RAISIN

1 slice pumpernickel raisin bread
4 tbsp. chunky peanut butter
1 small banana, 2-3 thin vertical slices
1 slice pumpernickel raisin bread, spread with 2 tbsp. peanut butter

....

STEAK SANDWICH

Long, soft, seeded baguette roll, cut in half; grill the open sides of the roll and spread both sides with spicy mustard

Fill with:
4 thin slices London Broil, cooked to taste
1 slice Alpine Lace Swiss cheese
1 Kosher garlic pickle, sliced vertically into 3 pieces

....

EGG 'N MUFFIN
(Recipe makes one stuffed muffin.)

1 oat bran English muffin, split (or any grain type you prefer)
2 strips cooked and drained bacon; (1 slice Canadian bacon or pepper ham)
1 slice cheese: sharp cheddar, Muenster or Alpine Lace Swiss
1 tbsp. hearty mustard spread
1 tbsp. pickle relish
1 cooked (not runny) poached egg (or use egg substitute in poaching cup);
    or 1 egg, scrambled into a patty (or use egg substitute)

Split English muffin and lightly toast. Spread mustard on one-half of muffin, and relish on the other half. Lay meat on mustard half. Top with egg and cover with slice of cheese. Close with relished muffin-half. Wrap in foil and heat thoroughly in preheated oven 400° for several minutes, until cheese starts to melt.

....

GRILLED BAY SCALLOPS AND ROASTED PEPPERS
ON A LONG SEEDED SOFT ROLL

1 (6-inch) seeded, soft roll, split
$\frac{1}{2}$ cup bay scallops, coated with 1 tbsp. olive oil, 1 tsp. balsamic vinegar,
    dash of black pepper, 1 tsp. chopped parsley, 1 garlic clove, minced,
    1 tsp. lemon juice (per sandwich)
$\frac{1}{2}$ red pepper, roasted, skin removed
      (see page 13 on "How to Roast Peppers")
red leaf lettuce

Sauté seasoned scallops in a small skillet for 1-2 minutes. Grill the inside halves of the roll; pack the scallops mix on one-half of the roll; add red pepper; add red leaf lettuce and press top half of roll in place.

....

GRILLED EGGPLANT AND TOMATO SANDWICH

1 (6-inch) soft baguette roll, split
2 thin slices eggplant (with skin) ¼-inch thick, basted with 1 tbsp. olive oil
     mixed with 1 tsp. balsamic vinegar and sprinkled with black pepper
3 very thin slices beefsteak tomatoes
¼ cup baby spinach, rinsed and drained
2 tbsp. shredded mozzarella

Baste eggplant with oil-vinegar mix; grill on both sides until lightly browned.
Grill soft sides of split baguette. Add eggplant slices and tomato slices; pack
spinach on top of sandwich half and sprinkle with mozzarella. Close with top
half of baguette; insert 2 wet wooden toothpicks into sandwich to hold it
together. Place on sheet of foil in preheated oven 450° F for 2-3 minutes to
melt cheese.

....

SALMON SALAD AND SLICED EGG ON A ROLL

1 small can (about 6-8 oz.) Alaska wild salmon
½ cup chopped celery
2 tbsp. mayonnaise
2 hard cooked large eggs, shelled, sliced
½ cup shredded carrot
4 thin slices tomato
1 tbsp. mayonnaise and 2 tsp. mustard spread, blended

2 Kaiser rolls, split

Prepare salmon salad by mixing salmon, celery and mayonnaise. Pack mix into
bottom halves of each roll; layer with sliced egg over salmon; then, press
shredded carrots on eggs; top with slices of tomato. Close with top half of
roll; spread with mayonnaise-mustard mix. Serve with a side of pitted olives.
(Makes 2 healthy stuffed rolls.)

....

THREE WRAPS

Ready-made wheat or vegetable tortillas (usually sold in packages of 10 in fresh food department or deli)

½ tomato, thinly sliced
shredded lettuce
Dressings: mayonnaise, mustard, chili relish

a) thin sliced chicken breast, grilled
    slice of pepper ham

b) thinly shaved cooked, medium-rare roast beef
    2 slices jalapeño Monterey Jack cheese

c) thin sliced cooked turkey breast
    2 slices Virginia ham

Sprinkle both sides of tortilla with water. Lay them on a metal baking sheet. In a preheated oven 400° F, warm tortillas for 2 minutes. Remove from oven. Spread tortillas with dressing. Neatly arrange ingredients of your choice on each tortilla. Roll stuffed tortillas and use a toothpick to hold it all together. You may wish to warm the prepared wraps in a hot oven for 2 minutes. Serve immediately.

....

BAGEL WITH CREAM CHEESE AND SMOKED SALMON

1 bagel, cut in half; on bottom half spread:

3-4 tbsp. low-fat cream cheese
3-4 thin slices smoked salmon
1 tsp. capers
4 tsp. horseradish, (optional)

top with other half of bagel

....

BREADSTICKS WITH ASPARAGUS SPEARS AND PROSCIUTTO

6-12 long breadsticks (any flavor)
6-12 slender spears asparagus, trimmed, rinsed, drained
6-12 thin, shaved slices prosciutto
1 cup soft, spreadable cheese, (eg.) relish-cream cheese, soft cheddar, brie
2 tbsp. olive oil
2 tsp. balsamic vinegar

Spread cheese on breadsticks. Wrap one slice prosciutto around one breadstick and one asparagus spear, holding them together. Lay the breadstick wraps on a serving tray; brush them with a mix of oil and vinegar. Serve with a bowl of Beef Barley Soup (see page 10).
(This is a great picnic lunch any time of the year. Pack the soup in a large thermos or jug.)

....

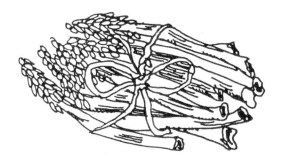

HEROES IN THE MAKING

ITALIAN HERO

1 large loaf (12-15 inches) seeded Italian bread, ends cut off (save to stale
    for crumbs)
6 slices Genoa salami
6 slices pepper ham
6 slices capicolla
6 slices sharp provolone
6 slices hot pepper cheese
6 thin slices beefsteak tomato
2 hot cherry peppers, seeded, quartered
½ cup pitted calamata olives, chopped
1 cup shredded lettuce
2 tbsp. olive oil
1 tbsp. red wine vinegar

Slice the loaf in half, lengthwise. Remove some of the soft bread from the
bottom half (save to stale for crumbs). Arrange the ingredients in layers,
from salami to shredded lettuce. Sprinkle with a mix of oil and vinegar. Place
top half of loaf over filling. Insert sandwich picks at 2-inch intervals to hold
hero in place. Wrap in foil and refrigerate to store until serving. Serves 4-6.

For a picnic or a tailgate, Three Bean Salad and Pasta (see page 28), or
Marinated Corn and Bean Salad (see page 60) make a satisfying
accompaniment.

....

SALAMI AND RED ONION ON ITALIAN WHOLE WHEAT HERO

1 loaf (12 inches) Italian whole wheat bread, ends removed (save to stale
    for crumbs)
18 slices Genoa salami
1 large red onion, thinly sliced in rounds
1 cup shredded lettuce
2 tbsp. olive oil
1 tbsp. red wine vinegar

Cut loaf in half and arrange ingredients in layers; sprinkle with a mix of
vinegar and oil. Insert sandwich picks every 2 inches to fasten hero. Wrap in
foil and refrigerate until needed. Serves 4.

....

SAUSAGE AND PEPPER HERO

1 loaf (12 inches) semolina bread, ends removed (save to stale for bread
    crumbs), cut in half, lengthwise
4 links Italian sweet sausages
¼ cup water
4 Italian fryer peppers, seeded, quartered
1 large onion, sliced in thin rounds
4 baby bella mushrooms, rinsed, quartered
2 tbsp. olive oil

Brown sausage in oil in skillet at 300° F; add water after cooking for
4-5 minutes; cover. Lower to 180° F and simmer for a few minutes; add
onions, peppers and mushrooms. Remove lid and sauté sausages and
vegetables until vegetables are tender and sausages are cooked through.
Remove some soft bread from bottom half of loaf (save to stale for bread
crumbs). Spoon the cooked sausages and vegetables into the bottom half of
loaf-include the gravy. Lay the top half of the loaf in place; fasten the hero
with sandwich picks every 2 inches. Wrap in foil; keep warm.
Serve warm. Serves 4.

．．．．．．．．．．．．．．．．．．．．．．．．．．．．．．．．．．．．．

VEAL CUTLET AND PEPPER HERO

1 loaf (12-15 inches) seeded Italian
    bread, ends removed (save to
    stale for crumbs)
4 medium-large veal cutlets,
    pounded thin
1 large egg (or egg substitute)
    beaten
½ cup unseasoned crumbs

¼ tsp. black pepper
1 tbsp. chopped parsley
4 Italian fryer peppers, seeded,
    quartered
1 onion, sliced in thin rounds
1 large beefsteak tomato, sliced in
    thin rounds
4 tbsp. olive oil

Dip cutlets in beaten egg; coat with crumbs, mixed with pepper and parsley.
Sauté breaded veal in hot oil in large skillet at 300° F for 2-3 minutes on
each side. Remove to platter and keep warm. Add peppers and onion to
skillet and sauté at 300° F, moving vegetables with spatula and cook to
lightly brown. Remove some soft bread from bottom half of loaf (save to
stale for crumbs). Stuff the loaf with cutlets, topped with pepper and
onions. Add a layer of sliced tomatoes. Cover with top half of loaf and
insert sandwich picks at 2-inch intervals to fasten hero. Wrap in foil; keep
warm until serving. Serves 4-6. (Serve with Hot Potato Salad, see page 112,
as an accompaniment.)

．．．．．．．．．．．．．．．．．．．．．．．．．．．．．．．．．．

MEATBALL HERO

Prepare: Sausage and Meatball Tomato Sauce (see page 187). OMIT the sausages. Follow recipe directions for making meatballs; however, for the hero, form $1\frac{1}{2}$-inch meatballs and prepare HALF of the recipe:

1 lb. chopped beef
$\frac{1}{4}$ cup unseasoned crumbs
1 tsp. chopped parsley

dash of salt and black pepper
1 beaten egg or $\frac{1}{4}$ cup egg
   substitute

Follow the remainder of the recipe and save the sauce for a BAKED ZITI which could make a festive accompaniment for this Meatball Hero. (See below.)

HERO:
1 (12-inch) loaf semolina bread, cut in half; remove ends and some of the
   soft bread from bottom half of the loaf (save to stale for crumbs)
1 dozen small meatballs, cooked in sauce, as directed in recipe
$\frac{1}{4}$ cup grated Parmesan cheese
1 cup baby spinach, rinsed, drained

Stuff the bottom half of loaf with meatballs and sauce; sprinkle with cheese; top with baby spinach. Cover with top half of loaf and fasten with sandwich picks at 2-inch intervals. Wrap in foil to keep warm. Serve warm; serves 4-6.

BAKED ZITI

Recipe for Sausage and Meatball Tomato Sauce (see page 187). After you remove the meatballs with some sauce, set rest of sauce aside in saucepot.

1 lb. cut ziti
1 cup grated Parmesan cheese
1 cup shredded mozzarella

Prepare pasta al dente or as directed on package. Cook pasta for one minute less than recommended by the manufacturer; drain; rinse in cool water; drain again. Transfer to large bowl. Pour half of the remaining sauce into bowl with pasta. Toss to coat thoroughly. Pour into 9x15 oven-proof casserole (or lasagna pan). Spoon rest of sauce over casserole; sprinkle with grated cheese and mozzarella. Bake in preheated oven 375° F for 25-30 minutes, until bubbly. Serves 6. (If you add one of the many greens salads from LUNCH IS IN THE BAG!, you'll enjoy a festive lunch at home or away. Both the hero and pasta may be wrapped in foil and warmed on a low grill.)

....

FRITTATA HEROES

1 loaf (12-15 inches) seeded Italian bread, cut in half lengthwise, ends removed, and some soft bread removed from bottom half (save to stale for crumbs)

Stuff bread with a frittata of your choice (see recipes below). Serves 3-4. May be wrapped in foil and reheated .

FRITTATA RECIPES

(For best results, use 9-inch Teflon or non-stick skillets with lids.)

1 tsp. olive oil
6-8 large eggs for each frittata (or, 1 $\frac{1}{2}$ – 2 cups egg substitute)
$\frac{1}{4}$ tsp. salt
$\frac{1}{8}$ tsp. black pepper
1 tbsp. chopped basil
1 tsp. oregano

Select from the following list of ingredients and prepare in advance:

Mushroom and Onion
    4 chopped mushrooms and 1 chopped onion
    Sauté 4 chopped mushrooms in 1 tbsp. olive oil. Add 1 chopped onion. Toss to cook. After 2 to 3 minutes transfer to bowl.

Peppers
    4 seeded and sliced frying peppers, sautéed al dente
    Sauté 4 green fryers in 1 tbsp. olive oil until tender, tossing occasionally. Transfer to bowl.

Asparagus
    6 stalks asparagus, trimmed, cut in 2-inch pieces, sautéed al dente
    Sauté asparagus pieces in 3 tbsp. olive oil for 3-4 minutes, tossing occasionally. Transfer to bowl.

Ham and Olives
    $\frac{1}{2}$ cup cubed ham, $\frac{1}{4}$ cup chopped pimiento olives
    Chop ham into small cubes; add chopped pimiento.

Zucchini
    2 small zucchini thinly sliced in rounds; sauté al dente
    Scrub zucchini, slice thin rounds (do not pare), sauté in 1 tbsp. olive oil, tossing at times, for 4-5 minutes. Transfer to bowl.

Potato

1 large pared, cooked, sliced potato, 1 small onion, chopped
Boil potato in jacket for 20 minutes. Peel off skin and slice into rounds.
Sauté potato slices and 1 chopped onion in 2 tbsp. oil for 3-4 minutes.
Transfer to bowl.

Italian Cheeses

$\frac{1}{2}$ cup each: grated Parmesan cheese, cubed mozzarella

Preheat lightly oiled skillet at 300° F. Beat 6-8 eggs with $\frac{1}{8}$ tsp. black
pepper and $\frac{1}{4}$ tsp. salt until thick and foamy. Pour the egg mixture into hot
oiled skillet. When the eggs start to set, add the prepared frittata
ingredients of your choice from above. Cover with lid. When omelet is set
and firm, loosen with spatula and invert onto a large platter and then back to
the skillet to cook the other side of the frittata, about 2 minutes longer.
Slide from skillet to serving platter. Fit into prepared loaf and add top-half
of loaf. Serve warm.

For variety try:
(1) Add 1 cup cooked shrimp halved, to the egg mix. Use a 5-inch skillet and
cook up a batch of shrimp omelets. Stack them in groups of threes. Between
each frittata, ladle Curry Sauce (see page 180). This makes an excellent
Egg Foo Yung.

OR

(2) Add 1 cup spicy sausage rounds to egg mix. First, cook sausage rounds in
skillet; then pour egg mix over them and cook to set. Prep two different
cheese omelets (e.g. Provolone, Asiago, Mozzarella or Gruyere) and alternate
cheese/sausage/cheese omelets in a stack. Serve with Marinara Sauce
(see pages 185-6).

....

ANTIPASTO AND MORE
(Prepare early on the day.)

3 round serving trays or platters, each: 12-15 inches in diameter
3 glass bowls, ½-pt. each (3 pint-size glass jars for storing)
2 bread baskets, lined with colorful napkins
2 small loaves artisan bread: roasted garlic, olive mix, pecan raisin,
    whole grain

PREPARE THE SEASONED DIPPING OILS :

(1)
½ cup extra virgin
    olive oil
2 tbsp. balsamic
    vinegar
1 tbsp. chopped sun
    dried tomatoes
1 tbsp. crushed dried
    rosemary
2 garlic cloves,
    minced
dash of salt
⅛ tsp. coarsely
    ground black
    pepper

(2)
½ cup extra virgin
    olive oil
2 tbsp. pitted,
    chopped Sicilian
    olives
2 garlic cloves,
    minced
1 tsp. black
    peppercorns
1 tsp. each: dried
    oregano, chopped
    fresh basil
1 bay leaf (whole)

(3)
½ cup extra virgin
    olive oil
juice of 1 lemon,
    strained
1 tsp. grated lemon
    peel
2 garlic cloves,
    minced
1 tsp. black
    peppercorns
1 tsp. capers
1 tsp. dried oregano

Store each recipe of seasoned dipping oils in separate glass 1-pint jars with screw-top lids. Shake well. Set aside. At serving time, shake the oils to blend thoroughly; pour each mix into separate glass serving bowls. Set the bowls upon one large serving tray. Slice the breads into chunks, 1x3-4 inches, just before serving. Arrange the bread in bread baskets and place adjacent to the tray of oils.

....

PREPARE THE ANTIPASTO TRAYS:

(Tray 1)

15 slices spicy capicolla

sharp provolone, cut into 15 finger-size sticks

15 slices Genoa salami (with peppercorns)

ricotta salata, cut into 15 finger-size sticks

2 hard, ripe beefsteak tomatoes, sliced in thick rounds, halved

1 can (1 lb.) unseasoned artichokes, halved

1 cup assorted pitted olives

sprigs of basil for garnish

Wrap one slice of capicolla around one stick of provolone. Wrap one slice salami around a stick of ricotta salata. Repeat until meats and cheeses are paired. Arrange them in a circle around the edge of one large round tray. Spoon the olives into the center of the tray leaving a circular space between the olives and roll-ups for the sliced tomatoes. Garnish with basil and artichokes.

(Tray 2)

1 large ripe, scented honeydew melon (or cantaloupe), cut into narrow wedges, about 12-15 slices, skin removed. (Wash melon under running water; and dry with paper towels, before handling.)

15 slices prosciutto

** 2 avocados, pared, pitted, sliced vertically; sprinkle with lemon juice

2 oranges, navel or tangelo, sliced into rounds, with skin, halved.

(Wash oranges under running water; dry with paper towels before slicing.)

8 fresh figs, washed, trimmed, halved

$\frac{1}{2}$ pt. blackberries, gently rinsed, drained

2 kiwi, pared, sliced in rounds

sprigs of mint (if available) for garnish

**YOU MAY PREPARE AN AVOCADO DIP INSTEAD: remove skin and pits from avocados: in a small bowl, thoroughly mash avocados with 1 tbsp. mayonnaise, 1 tsp. chili powder, 1 tbsp. lemon juice; mound avocado dip in center of platter (instead of blackberries); strew blackberries around platter. Sprinkle avocado dip with chili powder/finely chopped cilantro. Serve with a small basket of cracker crisps.

Wrap one slice of prosciutto around one wedge of melon. Arrange all of the melon/prosciutto wedges around the edge of the tray. Mound the berries in center of tray (or strew around platter); or mound avocado dip in center of tray. Garnish with halved figs, orange slices, kiwi, (avocado slices), and sprigs of mint.

Entire assembly generously and elegantly serves 4-6. A sweet Reisling or a light Sangiovese makes a suitable accompaniment.

ACCOMPANIMENTS:

DRESSINGS, SAUCES, GRAVIES

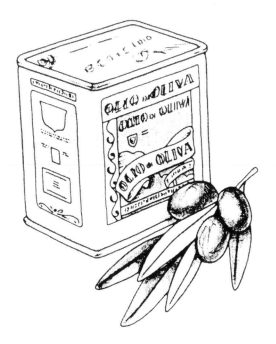

ITALIAN DRESSING

$\frac{1}{2}$ cup olive oil
2 tbsp. red wine vinegar
2 garlic cloves, crushed
$\frac{1}{4}$ tsp. salt
$\frac{1}{8}$ tsp. black pepper
1 tbsp. chopped basil
$\frac{1}{4}$ tsp. oregano flakes
a few flakes hot red pepper

Combine all ingredients in a 1-pint jar with a tight lid. Shake vigorously. Let stand 1 hour in refrigerator. Shake well before serving. Keeps in refrigerator for 2 weeks.

....

BALSAMIC OLIVE OIL DRESSING

$\frac{1}{2}$ cup olive oil
$\frac{1}{4}$ cup balsamic vinegar
1 tbsp. mixed: dried oregano, basil, rosemary, marjoram
1 bay leaf
2 garlic cloves, minced
1 tsp. honey
1 tsp. prepared Dijon-style mustard
few grains hot red pepper flakes

Combine all ingredients in a 1-pint jar with a tight cap. Shake well. Refrigerate. Shake well before using. Keeps for about 2 weeks in refrigerator.

....

HONEY MUSTARD DRESSING

$\frac{1}{2}$ cup olive oil
$\frac{1}{4}$ cup red wine vinegar (for sweeter taste, try cider vinegar)
1 tsp. honey
1 tsp. dry mustard
$\frac{1}{4}$ tsp. cracked black pepper
1 tsp. lemon juice
$\frac{1}{4}$ tsp. dill weed
salt to taste
Combine all ingredients a 1-pint jar with a tight cover. Shake thoroughly to combine. Refrigerate. Shake well to mix before serving. Keeps in refrigerator for 2 weeks.

....

FRENCH DRESSING

1 cup mayonnaise
1 tbsp. white vinegar
1 tsp. dry mustard
½ tsp. Worcestershire sauce
¼ tsp. salt
1 tsp. confectioners' sugar
½ tsp. paprika
¼ tsp. garlic powder
dash of black pepper

Combine all ingredients in a small bowl. Beat with electric mixer for 2 minutes. Pour into 1-pint jar with a secure cover. Refrigerate until serving. Stir thoroughly to mix. Keeps in refrigerator for 1 week.

....

LEMON-OIL DRESSING

½ cup olive oil
¼ tsp. salt
1 garlic clove, crushed
juice of 2 lemons, strained
dash of black pepper

Combine all ingredients in a 1-pint jar with a tight cover. Shake well. Refrigerate until serving. Use over green salads; vegetables such as broccoli, asparagus, spinach, or green beans. Keeps in refrigerator for 2 weeks.

....

RUSSIAN DRESSING

1 cup mayonnaise
½ cup chili sauce
½ cup pickle relish
1 tsp. confectioners' sugar
1 tbsp. black caviar, optional

Combine all ingredients into a 1-pint jar with a tight lid. Stir to mix. Refrigerate until using. Keeps in refrigerator for 1 week.

....

BLEU CHEESE DRESSING (OR: ROQUEFORT, GORGONZOLA)

½ cup olive oil
¼ cup white vinegar
¼ tsp. salt
⅛ tsp. cracked black pepper
1 tsp. onion powder
½ cup crumbled bleu cheese (or Roquefort or gorgonzola)

Combine and beat all ingredients in a small bowl. Pour into a 1-pint jar with a wide mouth. When ready to serve, stir thoroughly and spoon over salad. Keeps in refrigerator for 1 week.

....

CAESAR DRESSING

¼ cup egg substitute
½ cup grated Parmesan cheese
¼ tsp. salt
⅛ tsp. cracked black pepper
¼ tsp. dry mustard
1 cup toasted cubes French bread (or
  prepared croutons)

½ cup olive oil
2 garlic cloves, minced
2 strips cooked bacon, crumbled
3-4 chopped anchovies, optional
juice of 1 lemon, strained

Let minced garlic sit in olive oil for 1 hour. Wash salad greens and drain; set aside in refrigerator. In a small bowl, beat the egg substitute, cheese, salt, pepper, dry mustard, and lemon juice. Add oil mix. Beat with mixer for 30 seconds. Refrigerate. When needed, shake well. Add croutons to salad mix and pour dressing over the salad. Toss to coat thoroughly. Serve immediately.

....

SPICY SALAD DRESSING

1 cup Miracle Whip dressing
¼ cup chili sauce
¼ tsp. salt
⅛ tsp. black pepper
¼ tsp. dill weed

1 tbsp. chopped dill pickle
1 tbsp. olive oil
1 tbsp. Worcestershire sauce
dash of cayenne pepper

Beat all ingredients in a small bowl. Store in a tightly covered jar in refrigerator until needed. Shake well before serving.

....

MAYONNAISE

½ cup egg substitute
2 tbsp. lemon juice (1 tbsp. white wine vinegar, if necessary)
1 tbsp. mild mustard
1 ¼ cups olive oil
dash of salt, dash of white pepper

In a small bowl, whisk together: egg substitute, dash of salt and white pepper.
Add 1 tablespoon of lemon juice and the mustard. Beat until thick (about a minute or two). Add the oil a teaspoon at a time, whisking constantly. After you've added 2 tablespoons of oil, the mixture should be thick. Add the remaining oil more quickly, a tablespoon at a time, whisking constantly. Taste, and if desired, stir in the rest of the lemon juice (and 1 tablespoon of white vinegar); add more salt and pepper, if necessary. Refrigerate in a covered jar.

....

ASIAN DRESSING

¼ cup olive oil
2 tbsp. sesame oil
2 tbsp. rice wine vinegar
1 tbsp. grated gingerroot
2 tbsp. soy sauce

2 tbsp. lemon juice
1 tbsp. grated lemon rind
¼ tsp. salt
1 garlic clove, minced
2 tbsp. peanuts, chopped fine

Combine all ingredients in a jar with a lid. Refrigerate until needed. Shake well before serving.

....

PARMESAN CHEESE DRESSING

½ cup olive oil
¼ cup white wine vinegar
2 tbsp. lemon juice
¼ tsp. black pepper
½ tsp. salt
1 tbsp. oregano
1 bay leaf
½ cup grated Parmesan cheese

Combine all ingredients in 1-pint jar with lid. Refrigerate until needed. Shake well before serving.

....

VINAIGRETTE

½ cup olive oil
2 tbsp. red wine vinegar
1 tbsp. lemon juice
1 tsp. prepared mustard (or
    Worcestershire sauce)
½ tsp. salt

1 tsp. dried basil
¼ tsp. black pepper
1 garlic clove, minced
¼ cup sour cream for creamy style
    (optional)

Mix all ingredients in a 1-pint jar with lid. Refrigerate. Shake well at serving.

……………………………..

AIOLI (GARLIC SAUCE)

½ cup mayonnaise
4 garlic cloves, minced
¼ cup olive oil

¼ tsp. black pepper
1 tbsp. lemon juice
dash of salt

Mix ingredients thoroughly in a small bowl. Seal with plastic and refrigerate until needed. Stir before using.

……………………………..

COLE SLAW DRESSING

½ cup Miracle Whip dressing
¼ cup cider vinegar
juice of 1 lemon

¼ tsp. black pepper
1 tsp. sugar
½ tsp. celery seed

Mix all ingredients in a small jar with lid. Refrigerate. Shake well before serving.

……………………………..

APPLE CIDER DRESSING

½ cup apple cider
¼ cup olive oil
1 tbsp. brown sugar
¼ tsp. ground cinnamon
¼ tsp. nutmeg
¼ tsp. cloves

dash of pepper
dash of salt
dash of cumin
1 tbsp. lemon juice
1 tbsp. Sherry wine

Mix all ingredients in a small jar with lid. Shake vigorously before serving.

……………………………..

MARINADE (FOR PORK, CHICKEN, AND FISH)

¼ cup olive oil
3 tbsp. chopped parsley
¼ tsp. cracked black pepper
¼ tsp. salt

1 tbsp. honey
2 tbsp. prepared mustard
juice of 1 lemon, strained

Combine all ingredients in a small bowl. Refrigerate until needed. Before cooking meat/chicken/fish, brush on both sides of pork, chicken or fish, prior to cooking. Refrigerate for 1 hour. While cooking, brush occasionally with marinade.

....

MORNAY SAUCE

4 tbsp. olive oil or butter
4 tbsp. flour
1 cup evaporated milk
½ tsp. salt
¼ tsp. black pepper
4 oz. grated Swiss cheese (or cheddar or Parmesan)
cayenne pepper to taste

Over medium heat, in a small saucepot, melt butter (or heat oil) and stir in flour to make a smooth blend. Over heat, stir in milk, pepper and salt. Blend in grated cheese, stirring constantly to make a smooth sauce. Sprinkle cayenne pepper. Proceed as directed in your recipe.

....

BÉARNAISE SAUCE

1 small onion. chopped fine
1 tbsp. dried tarragon, crushed
1 tbsp. chopped chervil (or parsley)
¼ cup dry white wine
2 tbsp. white wine vinegar

¼ cup olive oil
½ cup egg substitute
1 tbsp. cold water
½ tsp. salt
¼ tsp. black pepper

In top half of 1-quart size double boiler over hot water, whisk egg substitute. Add cold water, herbs, wine and wine vinegar, steadily whipping. Add the oil or butter a little bit at a time; continue to whisk until sauce is thickened and creamy. Season with salt and pepper. Should the sauce curdle, add another tablespoon of cold water. Remove from heat and whip vigorously.

....

BARBEQUE SAUCE

1 cup catsup
1 tbsp. white vinegar
$\frac{1}{4}$ cup orange juice
$\frac{1}{4}$ tsp. salt
$\frac{1}{8}$ tsp. Tabasco
1 tbsp. Worcestershire sauce
$\frac{1}{4}$ cup dark molasses
$\frac{1}{4}$ tsp. whole cloves
$\frac{1}{4}$ tsp. garlic powder
$\frac{1}{2}$ tsp. dry mustard
1 tbsp. olive oil
dash of black pepper

Simmer all ingredients in a small saucepan for 5 minutes. Use as directed in recipes.

....

CHEESE SAUCE

3 tbsp. olive oil
$\frac{1}{4}$ cup flour
1 $\frac{1}{2}$ cups whole milk or evaporated milk
1 cup grated cheddar cheese
$\frac{1}{2}$ tsp. salt
$\frac{1}{4}$ tsp. black pepper
$\frac{1}{2}$ tsp. dry mustard
1 tsp. onion powder
1 tsp. Worcestershire sauce
few drops Tabasco

Heat oil over low temperature and stir in flour. Add milk and rest of ingredients. Stir constantly over low heat until mix is creamy and starts to thicken. Serve hot as directed in recipes.

....

BASIC CURRY SAUCE

3 tbsp. olive oil
3 tbsp. flour
$\frac{1}{2}$ tsp. salt
$\frac{1}{4}$ tsp. black pepper
$\frac{1}{4}$ tsp. cardamom
$\frac{1}{4}$ tsp. cumin
$\frac{1}{4}$ tsp. curry powder
$\frac{1}{4}$ tsp. mace
$\frac{1}{2}$ tsp. ginger
1 cup whole milk or evaporated milk
1 onion, minced
$\frac{1}{2}$ cup chopped celery
$\frac{1}{2}$ cup apple, chopped, leave skin
1 cup stock (or use bouillon cubes)
1 tsp. grated lemon rind
$\frac{1}{2}$ cup sherry
a few whole cloves

In a 1-quart saucepan, warm oil over low heat. Stir in flour, salt, seasonings, spices and herbs. Stir well over low heat. Gradually add milk, stirring continuously until creamy. Add chopped onion, celery, apple, lemon rind and stock. Stir to mix. Cook until sauce starts to simmer, and thickens. Add sherry. Stir to blend. Pour over cooked chicken, lamb or seafood (from which you have gotten the stock). Stir to combine and continue as in recipe.

....

CHILI SAUCE

1 $\frac{1}{2}$ cups prepared tomato sauce
1 cup prepared beef gravy (or 1 beef bouillon cube dissolved in 1 cup hot water, mixed
    with 2 tbsp. flour dissolved in $\frac{1}{4}$ cup cold water)
$\frac{1}{2}$ cup chili sauce
1 small onion, chopped
1 tbsp. olive oil

Combine and mix all ingredients in a 1-quart sauce pan. Simmer for 10 minutes. Serve with meat, fish, poultry or vegetables.

....

HOLLANDAISE SAUCE

$\frac{1}{2}$ cup olive oil
3 beaten eggs or egg substitute
1 tbsp. lemon juice
1 tsp. sherry
few grains of red cayenne pepper

In top of a double boiler, heat olive oil and slowly stir in beaten eggs. Add lemon juice, sherry and cayenne. Stir constantly.
Do not make water boil in lower pot, just keep it warm. You may prepare sauce in advance. Upon removing it from refrigerator, simply warm the sauce over hot, not boiling, water, stirring constantly.

…………………………..

HAWAIIAN SWEET AND SOUR SAUCE

$\frac{1}{2}$ cup meat, poultry, seafood stock*
1 tsp. mustard powder
$\frac{1}{4}$ tsp. black pepper
$\frac{1}{2}$ cup dark corn syrup
1 tbsp. brown sugar
1 tbsp. soy sauce
1 tsp. cornstarch stirred into 2 tbsp. cold water
1 cup pineapple chunks
1 cup pineapple juice (or peach nectar)
$\frac{1}{2}$ cup green pepper, seeded, sliced
6 maraschino cherries, crushed

Combine all sauce ingredients in a small bowl. Pour over meat, fowl, or seafood which is cooking and continue to simmer for 10 to 15 minutes longer. Or, to saucepan, add some stock made from $\frac{1}{2}$ cup hot water and chicken bouillon or cooked seafood liquid; or Gravy Master dissolved in $\frac{1}{2}$ cup water. Add and simmer for 15 minutes as directed above.
*When cooking together with pork, chicken, or seafood, pour combined ingredients over the meat, fowl, or fish while cooking. Otherwise add $\frac{1}{2}$ cup chicken stock with bouillon, or shrimp stock; or 1 tsp. Gravy Master in $\frac{1}{2}$ cup water as a stock.

…………………………..

CHINESE BARBEQUE SAUCE
(For pork, beef, shrimp, ribs or chicken.)

3 tbsp. olive oil
1 tbsp. peanut oil
3 scallions, chopped
2 garlic cloves, minced
1 small onion, chopped
1 tbsp. cornstarch stirred into $\frac{1}{4}$ cup
    cold water
1 cup stock (if none is available, use
1 tbsp. Gravy Master dissolved in
    1 cup water)

1 tbsp. soy sauce
1 tbsp. hoisin sauce*
$\frac{1}{4}$ cup plum sauce
$\frac{1}{2}$ cup catsup
1 tsp. grated gingerroot
$\frac{1}{4}$ cup honey
3 tbsp. creamy peanut butter
1 tbsp. rice vinegar

Heat oils in 1-quart saucepan; sauté garlic and onion and scallions. Stir in cornstarch mixed with water. Add remaining ingredients and stir over low heat until peanut butter is melted. Use to baste and/or as a barbeque sauce in Chinese recipes.

*Hoisin and plum sauces may be purchased at supermarkets in Asian food sections.

…………………………..

MUSHROOM SAUCE

3 tbsp. olive oil
3 tbsp. flour
$\frac{1}{2}$ tsp. salt
$\frac{1}{4}$ tsp. black pepper
1 cup whole milk or evaporated milk
$\frac{1}{2}$ cup mushroom stock
1 tbsp. chopped onion
1 tbsp. Worcestershire sauce
1 cup mushrooms, scrubbed, sliced

Simmer mushrooms in water for 1 minute. Drain water and set aside. In 1-quart saucepan, heat oil and stir in flour until smooth. Add milk and stock water and seasonings, onions, and Worcestershire sauce. Stir constantly over low heat until smooth. Add mushrooms and stir to blend. Cook for another minute. Keep warm over a pan of hot water until ready to serve.

…………………………..

PESTO SAUCE

2 cups fresh basil leaves, washed, drained
6 cloves, garlic
1 oz. pignola (pine nuts)
½ cup grated Parmesan cheese
½ cup olive oil
salt, black pepper to taste

Combine all ingredients in food processor. Purée for 30 seconds or until basil leaves are creamed. Serve immediately, or pour into a 1-pint plastic container and freeze until needed. If frozen, transfer to refrigerator early on the day and when needed, warm container, lid removed, over a pan of hot water. Stir the sauce occasionally while warming. Serve with pasta or rice. Toss to coat.

....

BASIC BROWN GRAVY
(For meat and poultry; about 2 cups.)

3 tbsp. olive oil
¼ cup flour
½ cup prepared tomato sauce
1 tsp. Gravy Master
½ tsp. salt
¼ tsp. black pepper
1 onion chopped
Meat or fowl drippings plus water to make 1 ½ cups stock*
dash of red cayenne pepper

Brown onion in oil. Stir flour into the cold water and add stock, tomato sauce, Gravy Master, salt, pepper and cayenne. Stir into oil mix. Cook over low heat until sauce thickens. Keep warm over pan of hot water.

*If no drippings are available, use 2 beef or chicken bouillon cubes dissolved in 1 ½ cups hot water.

....

MUSHROOM TOMATO SAUCE
(May be prepared 2 to 3 days in advance and refrigerated; or freeze for several weeks.)

1 lb. mushrooms, scrubbed, thinly sliced
3 cups tomato purée
½ tsp. salt
¼ tsp. black pepper
1 garlic clove, minced
1 small onion, chopped
3 tbsp. olive oil
¼ tsp. each: fresh basil, parsley, dried thyme

In a 2-quart saucepot, sauté onion and garlic and mushrooms in olive oil over medium heat. When very lightly browned (about 2 minutes) add purée, spices and herbs. Simmer gently for 30 minutes. Serve over pasta or rice or use to accompany beef or fowl.

…………………………..

CHOPPED BEEF TOMATO SAUCE
(May be prepared and refrigerated for several days, or frozen for several weeks.)

3 tbsp. olive oil
2 lbs. lean chopped beef
2 garlic cloves, minced
1 onion, chopped
3 cups tomato purée
¼ cup water
½ tsp. salt
¼ tsp. black pepper
½ tsp. each: fresh basil. oregano, thyme, rosemary
½ cup Parmesan cheese, grated
½ cup red table wine
few grains hot red pepper flakes

Brown onion and garlic and chopped beef in hot oil, stirring occasionally to maintain beef in small chunks. Add remaining ingredients; stir to combine; slowly simmer with lid loosely covering pot of sauce. Simmer gently for 1 hour. Serve over pasta or rice.

…………………………..

MARINARA SAUCE
METHOD I

4-5 lbs. fresh, ripe plum tomatoes
1 can (6 oz.) tomato paste (if sauce
    needs to be thickened)
3 tbsp. olive oil
½ tsp. salt
1 tbsp. mixed: oregano, thyme, rosemary
¼ tsp. black pepper

1 tbsp. fresh chopped basil
1 green pepper, seeded, chopped
½ cup grated Parmesan cheese
2 garlic cloves, minced
1 small onion, chopped
Few grains hot red pepper flakes

In a 4-quart saucepot, heat oil; brown garlic and onion. Set aside. Wash tomatoes and place in a 6-quart pot with cover. Add ¼ cup water; cover and bring to a boil. Simmer for about 5 minutes, until tomatoes are very soft. Drain and strain the tomatoes and liquid through a colander or sieve with a large, deep bowl underneath to catch the puréed tomatoes. Or use a food mill which separates the pulp from the skin and seeds. When using colander, use your hands to push the tomatoes through. Discard the squeezed skins and seeds. Transfer the puréed sauce to the pot with the browned garlic and onion. Add the remaining ingredients and stir to mix. Simmer gently for 1 ½ hours with lid askew. (Stir in tomato paste as needed, if sauce is too loose.)

………………………………..

MARINARA SAUCE
METHOD II

2 lbs. canned plum tomatoes
1 green pepper, seeded, chopped
6 oz. can tomato paste
1 small onion, chopped
3 tbsp. olive oil
2 garlic cloves, minced

½ tsp. salt
½ cup grated Parmesan cheese
¼ tsp. black pepper
2-3 basil leaves
1 tbsp. mixed: oregano, rosemary, thyme
Few flakes hot red pepper

Strain plum tomatoes through a colander as in Method 1 or use blender. Brown garlic and onion in hot oil in a 2-quart saucepan with lid. Add puréed tomatoes, paste, and the remaining ingredients. Simmer gently, loosely covered for 1 ½ hours, stirring occasionally.

………………………………..

MARINARA SAUCE
METHOD III

3 cups canned tomato purée   2 garlic cloves, minced
3 tbsp. olive oil   1 small onion, chopped
½ tsp. salt   1 tbsp. mixed: oregano, rosemary, thyme
¼ tsp. black pepper   Few grains hot red pepper flakes
1 small green pepper, seeded, chopped   2-3 fresh basil leaves
½ cup grated Parmesan cheese

Brown onion and garlic in hot oil in a 2-quart saucepot with cover. Add tomato purée and remaining ingredients. Stir to mix and gently simmer, lightly covered, for 1 hour.

………………………………..

RAGOUT
(May be prepared up to 3 days in advance and refrigerated, covered, or may be frozen in a plastic container for several weeks.)

SAUCE:
large can plum tomatoes (about 3 cups), strained through colander
6 oz. can tomato paste
2 garlic cloves, minced
1 small onion, chopped
3 tbsp. olive oil
½ tsp. salt
¼ tsp. black pepper
1 tbsp. mixed: oregano, thyme, marjoram, rosemary
2-3 fresh basil leaves
½ cup red table wine
½ cup grated Parmesan cheese (or Pecorino Romano)
Few flakes hot red pepper

MEATS:
2 links sweet Italian sausage
2 links hot Italian sausage
1 lb. lean chopped beef (add 1 beaten egg, ½ cup fine crumbs, 1 tbsp. chopped parsley;
     optional: ¼ cup raisins)
½ lb. lean pork for gravy
1 thin slice top round for braccioli (meat should be pounded thin; add 1 tsp. chopped
     parsley, ¼ cup raisins and pignola, mixed; salt and pepper to taste)

(1) Preheat oil in 4-quart sauce pot to 300° F. Brown sausage and pork. Cook thoroughly. Remove from pot, set aside.

(2) Form meatballs by combining chopped beef, beaten egg, crumbs, salt, pepper and parsley. Form into 2-inch balls. Brown these in same skillet as sausage and pork. Set aside.

(3) Place thinly pounded top round on a sheet of waxed paper. Over it, sprinkle salt, pepper, parsley, raisins and pignola . Roll up and tie with white string or knit with a thin metal skewer to form braccioli. Brown the braccioli on all sides in skillet. Also brown onion and garlic. Scrape the bottom of the skillet to loosen leavings (which you add to meats).

(4) Replace all meats to saucepan and add all the sauce ingredients. Stir to combine thoroughly. Bring the pan to simmer, cover loosely, and cook the ragout for 1 hour. Serve the sauce over pasta or rice, with the meats as an accompaniment.

....

SAUSAGE AND MEATBALL TOMATO SAUCE
(May be prepared up to 3 days in advance and refrigerated, covered, or may be frozen in a plastic container for several weeks.)

MEAT:

3 links sweet Italian sausage

3 links hot Italian sausage

2 lbs. chopped beef for meatballs: add $\frac{1}{2}$ cup bread crumbs, 1 tbsp. chopped parsley, $\frac{1}{2}$ tsp. salt, $\frac{1}{4}$ tsp. black pepper and 1 beaten egg (or egg substitute)

3 tbsp. olive oil

3 garlic cloves, minced

1 small onion, chopped

In a skillet, brown sausages, onion and garlic in olive oil (300° F) until sausages are cooked. Remove meat to platter. In a 2-quart bowl, combine meatball ingredients and form 3-inch meatballs. Brown them in same skillet on all sides. Remove meatballs to platter. Scrape bottom of skillet to loosen leavings. In a large bowl, combine the following sauce ingredients:

SAUCE:

4 cups Italian plum tomatoes, strained or put through blender

$\frac{1}{2}$ cup tomato paste

$\frac{1}{2}$ tsp. salt

$\frac{1}{4}$ tsp. black pepper

2-3 fresh basil leaves

1 tbsp. mixed: oregano, rosemary, thyme, marjoram

$\frac{1}{2}$ cup Parmesan cheese

$\frac{1}{2}$ cup red table wine

Combine all meat and leavings in a 4-quart saucepan with cover. Add sauce ingredients and mix thoroughly. Simmer with lid askew for 1 $\frac{1}{2}$ hours, stirring occasionally. Serve sauce over pasta or rice. Serve meat as an accompaniment.

....

SEAFOOD TOMATO SAUCE
(May be prepared a day or two in advance and refrigerated.)

3 cups Italian plum tomatoes, strained or
    put through blender
2 tbsp. tomato paste
2 garlic cloves, minced
1 small onion, chopped
1 tbsp. chopped basil (or fresh mint)
1 tbsp. mixed: oregano, thyme,
    marjoram
1 bay leaf

$\frac{1}{2}$ tsp. salt
$\frac{1}{4}$ tsp. black pepper
$\frac{1}{2}$ cup dry white wine
3 tbsp. olive oil
2 cups raw, cleaned seafood (shrimp,
    crabs, clams, cleaned squid cut into
    rounds, mussels, lobsters-any one of
    these)
A few hot red pepper flakes

In a 4-quart saucepan with cover, sauté garlic and onion in oil (300° F) until lightly browned. Add other sauce ingredients, except seafood. Stir and simmer, covered, for 1 hour. Add cleaned seafood and simmer for an additional 10 minutes. Serve over spaghetti, linguini, or rice.
NOTE:
Clams: Use 1 cup chopped clams, plus the liquid which you should strain through a piece of cheesecloth or fine strainer.
Crabs or Lobsters: Use 6 small crabs or 1 whole lobster or 4 lobster claws.
Mussels: Scrub well. Add 1 dozen mussels in shell to sauce.
Shrimp: Clean, leave whole, about 1 lb.
Squid: Clean, cut into rounds. Use 2 cups.

…………………………..

RED PEPPER SAUCE
(May be prepared several days in advance and refrigerated or frozen.)

4 large red bell peppers
4 garlic cloves, peeled
1 cup tomato purée, unseasoned
1 small onion, chopped
1 hot chile pepper, chopped (careful
    handling)

$\frac{1}{4}$ cup olive oil
2 tbsp. balsamic vinegar
$\frac{1}{2}$ tsp. salt
$\frac{1}{4}$ tsp. black pepper
1 tsp. each: oregano, basil, rosemary
1-2 bay leaves, whole
$\frac{1}{2}$ cup grated Parmesan cheese

Wash peppers; remove the core and seeds. Cut the peppers into chunks and purée them in a food processor for a minute or so. Add the garlic and pulse for half a minute. In a medium saucepan with lid, add olive oil and brown the chopped onion and chile pepper (seeded and chopped). Cool slightly and add the puréed, red pepper and garlic. Add the tomato sauce, balsamic vinegar, and all the spices. Stir to mix. Return the pan with cover to the stove and simmer for 30 minutes, stirring occasionally. Stir in the grated cheese. Serve over pasta of your choice. Add more cheese if desired.

…………………………..

HAWAIIAN TOMATO SAUCE
(May be prepared a day in advance.)

1 cup prepared tomato sauce
1 tbsp. Gravy Master
½ cup pineapple juice
2 tbsp. brown sugar
1 tbsp. prepared mustard
½ cup pineapple chunks
½ cup green pepper, seeded, chopped
½ tsp. salt
¼ tsp. black pepper
1 tbsp. cornstarch stirred into ¼ cup cold water
1 tbsp. wine vinegar
Few dashes Tabasco

Combine all ingredients in a 1-quart saucepan. Simmer for 5 minutes.
Serve hot over rice.

………………………………..

INDEX

Berry, Very   134
Bleu Cheese Dressing   175
Blueberry Muffins   126

BREAD

Banana Bread   23
Breadsticks/Asparagus, Prosciutto   164
Cranberry Bread   114
Date Nut Bread   12
Ginger Muffins   17
Irish Soda Bread   38

Bread and Butter Pudding   11
Bread, Cranberry   114
Breadsticks/Asparagus, Prosciutto   164
Broccoli and Chick Pea Salad   24
Brochette of Scallops with Rice   78
Brown Gravy   183
Brownie Sundae   120

BRUNCHES

Chicken and Spinach   126
Chicken Pot Pie   122
French Toast/Ham, Cranberries   124
Ham in a Crust   137
Ham Steak and Corn Fritters   127
Pancakes, Happy Day   152
Poached Egg on Toast with Bacon 132
Polenta with Sausages and Bacon   130
Prosciutto and Cheese Quiche   139
Salmon Stew   135
Sausage Pie   134
Torta Rustica   129
Wheat Pasta, Bacon and Vegetables   141

Burger Soup   107
Butternut Squash Soup with Sausage   128

C

Cabbage Apple Slaw   38
Cabbage Slaw with Oranges   22
Caesar Dressing   175

CAKES

Almond Tart   29
Angelic Cake   107
Blueberry Muffins   126
Brownies   120
Candy-Cake   21
Cherry Coffee Cake   25
Chocolate Amaretto Cupcakes   101
Chocolate Pumpkin Muffins   99
Fruits in Batter   136
Ginger Muffins   17
Loaf of Chocolate, A   92
Pumpkin Cake   109
Trifle   32

Candy-Cake   21
Cannellini Bean Salad   83
Cantaloupe with Brandied Cherries   71
Caponata (Eggplant Stew)   66
Carrot, Chicory and Red Leaf Salad   100
Carrots, Glazed   113
Carrots, Green Beans, Provolone Salad   116
Cassoulet   5
Ceci and Gorgonzola Salad   90
Cheddar Cheese Soup   132

CHEESE

Ceci and Gorgonzola Salad   90
Cheddar Cheese Soup   132
Cheese Sauce   179
Escarole, Arugula with Ricotta Salata   62
Green Beans, Carrots, Provolone Salad   116
Parmesan Chicken   4
Parmesan Dressing   176
Pasta w/Chicken in 3-Cheese Sauce   100
Pear and Gorgonzola Salad   16
Prosciutto and Cheese Quiche   139
Provolone Soup   57
Sausage Pie   134
Spinach and Feta Salad w/Figs   95
Three Cheese Sauce   100
Tomato, Mozzarella and Figs   74
Torta Rustica   129

Cheese and Prosciutto Quiche   139
Cheese, Cheddar Soup   132
Cheese Sauce   179
Cheese (Three) Sauce   100
Chef's Salad   140

Cherry Coffee Cake   25
Cherry Noodle Pudding   19
Cherry-Raspberry Frappe   49
Chick Pea and Broccoli Salad   24

CHICKEN (FOWL)

Chicken and Pepper Ham Wrap   163
Chicken and Spinach   126
Chicken and Vegetable Soup   68
Chicken and Walnut Salad   58
Chicken Fingers Salad   64
Chicken Oregano   29
Chicken Parmesan   4
Chicken, Pasta and Artichokes   75
Chicken Piccata   2
Chicken Pot Pie   122
Chicken Ragout and Pasta   116
Chicken Sausage w/Pasta, Cheese   100
Chicken Teriyaki   51
Chicken Wings and Ribs   41
Cinnamon Chicken   93
Paella   22
Spicy Chicken with Vegetables   109
Turkey Scallopine   98
Turkey Tetrazzini   46
Waldorf Chicken Salad Sandwich   158

Chicken and Pepper Ham Wrap   163
Chicken and Spinach   126
Chicken and Vegetable Soup   68
Chicken and Walnut Salad   58
Chicken, Cinnamon   93
Chicken Fingers Salad   64
Chicken Oregano   29
Chicken Parmesan   4
Chicken, Pasta and Artichokes   75
Chicken Piccata   2
Chicken Pot Pie   122
Chicken Ragout and Pasta   116
Chicken Salad Sandwich (Waldorf)   158
Chicken Sausage,Pasta, 3-Cheese Sauce 100
Chicken, Spicy with Vegetables   109
Chicken Teriyaki   51
Chicken Wings and Ribs   41
Chicory, Red Leaf and Carrot Salad   100
Chili Sauce   180
Chinese Barbeque Sauce   182
Chocolate, A Loaf of   92
Chocolate Amaretto Cup Cakes   101
Chocolate Pumpkin Muffins   99

Chopped Beef Tomato Sauce   184
Cinnamon Chicken   93
Citrus in Marsala   3
Cobb Salad with Beets and Onions   72
Coffee Marshmallow Cream   84
Coffee Sorbet   56
Coffee Sundae   96
Cole Slaw Dressing   177

COOKIES

Almond Slices   7
Gingersnap Ice Cream Sandwiches   115
Macaroon Ambrosia   54
Stuffed Cookies   34

Corn and Bean Salad, Marinated   60
Corn Fritters   127
Corn Fritters with Ham Steak   127
Corn, Herbed and Tomato Chowder   87
Corn-on-the-Cob   58
Corned Beef Sandwich   157
Coupe Saint-André   67
Coupe Saint-Jacques   73
Crab Cakes   60
Cranberries with Curried Wild Rice   65
Cranberry Bread   114
Cranberry Sauce   124
Creole Lamb Chops   25
Croquettes, Salmon with Asparagus   67
Crostata, Apple, Walnuts, Cheddar   151
Crostata, 4-Cheese   149
Crostata, Pepperoni, Gorgonzola   151
Crostata/Provolone, Salami,Vegetables   147
Crostata, Sausage, Tomato   150
Crostata, Shrimp and Artichokes   146
Crostata, Sicilian   148
Crostata /Tomato, Broccoli, Prosciutto   150
Crostatas, 8   145 ff.
Crumbled Potato   27
Crust, (Crostata)   145
Crust, Pastry   122
Cucumber and Tomato Salad   88
Cup Cakes, Chocolate Amaretto   101
Curried Wild Rice and Cranberries   65
Curry Sauce   180
Curry Soup, Spicy Vegetables   40
Curry Veal   20

D

Date Nut Bread   12

DESSERTS

DRESSINGS

G

H

I

RICE

Asian Rice   17
Beans and Rice   21
Brochette of Scallops with Rice   78
Curried Wild Rice and Cranberries   65
Paella   22
Rice Custard, Autumn   125
Rice, Steamed   96
Rice with Cashews   36
Saffron Rice   79
Sweet and Sour Rice   9

Rice and Beans   21
Rice, Asian   17
Rice Custard, Autumn   125
Rice, Steamed   96
Rice with Cashews   36
Ricotta Salata/Escarole and Arugula   62
Roast Beef , Monterey Cheese Wrap   163
Roasted Baby Artichokes   91
Roasted Peppers   13
Roasted Salmon   49
Roasted Salmon Salad   64
Romaine/Apples, Red Onion, Black Olives 20
Rum Raisin, Frappe   117
Russian Dressing   174
Rustic Pasta   3

S

Saffron Rice   79

SALADS

Artichoke Hearts, Fennel , Arugula   30
Arugula, Radicchio and Endive   93
Asian Salad   50
Avocado Salad   81
Bean and Pepper Salad   98
Berry Fruit Waldorf Salad   129
Broccoli and Chick Pea Salad   24
Cabbage Apple Slaw   38
Cabbage Slaw with Oranges   22
Cannellini Bean Salad   83
Ceci and Gorgonzola Salad   90
Chef's Salad   140
Chicory , Red Leaf and Carrot   100

Chicken and Walnut Salad   58
Chicken Fingers Salad   64
Cobb Salad   72
Cucumber and Tomato   88
Egg Salad (Sandwich)   158
Eggs and Shrimp and Scallops   53
Escarole and Arugula/Ricotta Salata   62
Escarole, Frisée and Cashews   108
Fennel Salad   13
Figs, Oranges and Apples   125
Green Beans, Carrots and Provolone   116
Green Beans Salad   45
Greens, Mixed/Bleu Cheese Vinaigrette   106
Greens Salad w/ Pine Nuts and Olives   46
Hot Potato Salad on a Bed of Spinach   112
Latin Grill Salad   70
Lettuce and Tomato Salad/Ceci   118
Mandarin Orange Salad   78
Marinated Corn and Bean Salad   60
Mexican Scallops Salad   69
Mixed Greens Salad   2
Mixed Greens with Tarragon   55
Niçoise Salad   76
Pasta and Three-Bean Salad   28
Pear and Gorgonzola Salad   16
Red Cabbage and Apple Slaw   102
Red Cabbage, Cucumber, Radish, Tomato   26
Red Leaf, Radish and Pine Nuts   35
Red Potato,Green Beans,Roasted Pepper   85
Romaine/Apples, Onion, Black Olives   20
Roasted Salmon Salad   64
Salad of Greens and Carrots   6
Salad with Nuts and Fruit   8
Spinach and Feta Salad with Figs   95
Spinach, Endive Salad/Mandarin Oranges   18
Sweet and Sour Salad   48
Three-Bean Salad   28
Tomato and Avocado   133
Tomato, Mozzarella and Figs   74
Tomato, Onion and Bacon   131
Waldorf Chicken Salad Sandwich   158
Waldorf Salad/Grapes and Apples   104

Salami,Red Onion on Whole Wheat Hero   165
Salmon, Alaska, Pasta, Cheddar   154
Salmon Croquettes and Asparagus   67
Salmon, Roasted   49
Salmon Salad and Sliced Egg on a Roll   162
Salmon Salad, Roasted   64
Salmon (Smoked),Cream Cheese on a Bagel 163
Salmon Stew   135

Salmon with Pasta   62
Salsa   71

Seafood Jambalaya   56
Seafood Polenta   102
Seafood Stew   110
Seafood Stuffed Mushrooms   88
Seafood Tomato Sauce   188
Shrimp and Artichoke Crostata   146
Shrimp and Tuscan Pasta   72
Shrimp Scorpio   95
Shrimp Stuffed Mushrooms   144
Sicilian Crostata   148
Slaw, Cabbage-Apple   38
Slaw, Cabbage-Orange   22
Slaw, Red Cabbage-Apple   102
Smoked Ham, Turkey, Swiss on a Pita   158
Soda Bread, Irish   38
Sole Fillet, Baked   33

SOUPS

Avocado Soup   43
Beef Barley Soup   10
Burger Soup   107
Butternut Squash Soup/Sausage   128
Cheddar Cheese Soup   132
Chicken and Vegetable Soup   68
Corn (Herbed) and Tomato Chowder   87
Hot and Sour Soup   50
Oyster Stew   59
Pea Soup   149
Potage Saint-Jacques   33
Potato and Bacon Soup   97
Provolone Soup   57
Salmon Stew   135
Spicy Vegetable Curry Soup   40
Spring Soup   52

Soup, Hot and Sour   50
Spicy Apple Slices   12
Spicy Chicken and Vegetables   109
Spicy Salad Dressing   175
Spicy Vegetable Curry Soup   40
Spinach and Chicken   126
Spinach and Feta Salad with Figs   95
Spinach, Endive Salad/Mandarin Oranges   18
Spring Soup   52

STEWS

Bean Stew   82
Beef and Pork Stew   18
Beef Stroganoff   26

Caponata (Eggplant Stew)   66
Cassoulet (Beans)   5
Chicken Ragout and Pasta   116
Jambalaya w/ Seafood   56
Oyster Stew   59
Salmon Stew   135
Sausage Jambalaya   104
Seafood Stew   110

Stew, Bean   82
Stew, Beef and Pork   18
Stew, Oyster   59
Stew, Salmon   135
Stew, Seafood   110
Stewed Fruit   15
Stewed Fruit, Sweet and Tart   105
Stir-Fry Noodles   84
Stir-Fry Vegetables   41
Steak Sandwich   160
Strawberries, Oranges with Lime   45
Stroganoff, Beef   26
Stuffed Cookies   34
Stuffed Fish Fillets with Crabmeat   119
Stuffed Peaches   75
Stuffed Red Snapper, Stir-Fry Noodles   83
Sweet and Sour Rice   9
Sweet-Sour Salad   48
Sweet-Tart Stewed Fruit   105

T

Tapioca, Orange   103
Tarragon Dressing   55
Tart, Almond   29
Teriyaki Chicken   51
Tetrazzini, Turkey   46
Three-Bean Salad and Pasta   28
Tipsy Apple   27
Tipsy Pork   81
Tomato and Avocado Salad   133
Tomato and Cucumber Salad   88
Tomato and Lettuce Salad with Ceci   118
Tomato, Bacon, Peanut Butter Sandwich   157
Tomato, Broccoli, Prosciutto Crostata   150
Tomato, Mozzarella and Figs   74
Tomato, Onion and Bacon Salad   131
Torta Rustica   129
Trifle   32